Agricultural Reason in the Shadow of Subsistence Capitalism

HAU
Books

Director
Frédéric Keck

Editorial Collective
Deborah Durham
Casey High
Nora Scott

Managing Editor
Jane Sabherwal

Hau Books are published by the
Society for Ethnographic Theory (SET)

www.haubooks.org

Agricultural Reason in the Shadow of Subsistence Capitalism

A Rural Ontology from Western India

Arjun Appadurai

Hau Books

Chicago

Cover design: Daniel Meucci
Layout design: Deepak Sharma, Prepress Plus Technologies
Typesetting: Prepress Plus Technologies (www.prepressplustechnologies.com)

ISBN: 978-1-914363-06-1 [paperback]
ISBN: 978-1-914363-10-8 [PDF]
LCCN: 2024934007

Hau Books
Chicago Distribution Center
11030 S. Langley Ave.
Chicago, IL 60628
www.haubooks.org

Hau Books publications are marketed and distributed by The University of
Chicago Press.
www.press.uchicago.edu

Printed in the United States of America on acid-free paper.

Contents

Acknowledgments

I am grateful to the Board of HAU Books for supporting my interest in republishing this set of essays, most of them originally published in the 1980s. I owe a special debt of gratitude to Hylton White and Kriti Kapila, for their steadfast encouragement. Akhil Gupta read most of these essays in the original versions and encouraged me to turn them into a book over the years. I am especially thankful to Deborah Durham, who helped me to put together the whole book, oversaw copy editing, compiled the index, and made sure it was turned into a coherent manuscript. My young colleague Sandeep Mertia did the yeoman work of getting publishers' permissions, scanning the originals, converting them to Word documents, and making the transition to HAU style requirements much easier than it would otherwise have been.

It is also a pleasure to thank the many scholars who were my interlocutors during my original fieldwork and in the process of writing and publishing these essays. Among them are: Pranab Bardhan, Valentine Daniel, William Hanks, Akhil Gupta, Frédérique Apffel-Marglin, Dilip Menon, A. K. Ramanujan, Ashok Rudra, Lee Schlesinger, Amartya Sen, Anne Sharman, Brian Spooner, T. N. Srinivasan, and S. J. Tambiah.

Apart from the new introduction, the chapters in this book have been previously published. They have been edited for style, and some place names have been updated. What is now called Pune was, in the past spelled Poona, and throughout this text it is named Pune. References to Bombay have also been revised to the current Mumbai.

CHAPTER 1, *Andāj*, was previously published in a shorter version in *Changing Theory: From the Global South*, edited by Dilep Menon (London: Routledge India, 2022).

CHAPTER 2, Small-Scale Techniques and Large-Scale Objectives, was previously published in *Conversations Between Economists and Anthropologists*, edited by Pranab Bardhan (New Delhi: Oxford University Press, 1989).

CHAPTER 3, Wells in Western India: Irrigation and Cooperation in an Agricultural Society, was originally published, with several photographs not included here, in *Expedition* 26, 3 (1984). Reprinted here courtesy of the Penn Museum.

CHAPTER 4, Dietary Improvisation in an Agricultural Economy, was previously published in *Diet and Domestic Life in Society*, edited by Anne Sharman, Janet Theophano, Karen Curtis, and Ellen Messer (Philadelphia: Temple University Press; ©1991 by Temple University. All Rights Reserved).

CHAPTER 5, Technology and the Reproduction of Values in Rural Western India, was previously published in *Dominating Knowledge: Development, Culture and Resistance*, edited by Frédérique Apffel Marglin and Stephen A. Marglin (Oxford: Clarendon Press, 1991).

Introduction

Subsistence Capitalism

I have wondered for some decades about how to capture the best way to name the capitalism that links small holdings, rural inequality, commercialization, and poverty in societies like India for the last century and a half, and well into the present. I chose the term subsistence capitalism for an example of this type of regime in a village in Western India, which I call Vadi and where I did fieldwork in 1981–82. Capitalism in agrarian communities like it appears in numerous forms. One is the need for money, which spurs risky forms of cash cropping and debt incursion for irrigation and household consumption, migration to cities for factory jobs, petty commerce, and low-tech services like auto-rickshaws. Urban markets for grains, vegetables, and other crops, based on commercial capital in the hands of money-lenders, large agrarian merchants, and transport operators, are another capitalist feature. The third is the wage economy for poor farmers and land laborers, which is perennially tilted towards bare-life wages embedded in various historical and cultural forms of inequality. I use the term subsistence to refer to the fact that ninety percent of the farmers in villages such as the one I studied operate at the very edge of their needs for social reproduction, in terms of food, shelter, health, and socially necessary expenditures. Since overall agricultural productivity in such communities is low, the presence of capitalist commercialization is insufficient to lift all but a tiny portion of the population above the level of bare subsistence. These are the main reasons for my use of the term "subsistence capitalism" to characterize the village described in the following five essays, which are being re-printed together for the first time here.

The roads to this state of affairs in agrarian India are many, depending on whether one is in a semi-arid part of Rajasthan or Andhra Pradesh, a riverine valley such as that of the Kaveri or the Brahmaputra, a water-rich ecosystem as in parts of Goa, Kerala, or Bengal, an urban periphery in Telangana, or a remote rural location in Chhattisgarh. Further varia-tion comes from uneven transportation links and networks, unequal ac-cess to education, loans, and health facilities, and differential distances to market towns. Rural politics can also affect the trajectory of agrarian communities, which have different points of articulation between domi-nant castes in villages and caste politics at the district and state levels, differences which can either entrench or loosen local agrarian inequality.

But the remarkable fact of rural India is that all roads lead, not to Rome, but to a state of affairs which is characterized by high levels of discrimination towards Untouchable/Dalit castes, persistent bias against women, high levels of agrarian poverty, and a striking persistence of small holdings and quasi-feudal political structures. Almost 50 percent of India's total population consists of small farmers and their families, and 85 percent of all farms are smaller than two square hectares. Almost all the other indicators of welfare and well-being in rural India reflect these dismal statistics. This overall picture, of limited productivity, small holdings, and minimal mechanization of farming, is all the more striking because of its relative imperviousness to change. In dry villages like Vadi (which are the majority of poorly irrigated, fragmented, low-tech villages in India), 2022–23 is remarkably like 1981–82, except for the disturb-ing and deeper inroads of state-subsidized capitalism. This development itself has a deeper history.

In the nineteenth century, British administrator-scholars, such as Alexander Munro (1806), and the Britain-based social thinkers Henry Maine (1871) and Karl Marx (1853), all bemoaned the isolation, self-sufficiency, and changelessness of India's villages. This picture, which is still shared by many of us in the Indian elite, flies in the face of a large body of scholarship which has shown that for centuries before the arrival of the British, Indian villages were major nodes in a continental and even global network of commerce, trade, and industry (Perlin 1983). India's villages were quite dynamic and often came into being because groups of various kinds were seeking better lives and were thus "colonizing" new areas of India's countryside and setting up communities. After all, India did not become a land of six hundred thousand villages overnight. India's villages were also sites of mobility, conflict, and turbulence, and frequently provided soldiers, taxes, and skills to the entire country. Indian well-diggers, construction workers, artisans, and traders were incessantly on the move, creating networks of infrastructure and commerce from Tirupati to Nathdwara, and from Surat to Murshidabad. And these networks also brought India's villages into contact with the Indian Ocean, the Bay of Bengal, and with the lands west of the subcontinent, in today's Afghanistan and Iran. Great confederations of merchants linked the villages of Tamil Nadu to the lands of Southeast Asia during the Chola period (Stein 1977), a millennium before the Nattukottai Chettiars did something similar in Burma (Rudner 1994). And that is not counting other mercantile and artisanal groups who linked India's villages to regional and global economies.

In short, India was not always a land of isolated, static, and self-sufficient villages, but many changes in the eighteenth and nineteenth centuries, both ideological and infrastructural, pushed India's agrarian world into a sort of isolation and economic inertia which was not a part of their longer history. British colonial rulers—along with their Indian collaborators—were the reason for this delinking of India's villages from larger world economies, except as producers of cheap agricultural commodities and of an urban class of informalized, precarious, and exploited labor. Indian urban histories like that of Mumbai's brief period of industrial glory in the period from 1930 to 1980, which created something like a serious urban working class, with secure jobs, housing, and unions, represent a relatively short moment in Indian history, when the economic isolation of Indian villages was compensated by real urban possibilities.

Today's Indian villages are the targets of two less-than-benign forces, the state and the urban capitalist sector, which are in fact closely connected. Jamie Cross (2014), Michael Levien (2018), and Sai Balakrishnan (2019) have offered a compelling picture of the aggressive entry of urban and global commercial interests into agrarian land markets, through such devices as Special Economic Zones and development corridors, exemptions and licenses, enabled by the state. These scholars show how urban capitalists are racing into the agrarian land markets in order to build everything from malls and universities to factories and housing estates, at an alarming rate. In this, the urban capitalists are assisted directly by what Levien calls "the broker-state," that is, a local and central bureaucracy which acquires the land of farmers through a series of executive fiats, often at low prices, and then makes it available to these external capitalist interests. In the process, a vast amount of legal and illegal revenue is generated by officials of the state at every level, and nevertheless prime agricultural land is made available relatively cheaply for urban exploitation. This process stands in marked contrast to the developmentalist state of the Nehruvian era, which acquired agricultural land primarily for developmental projects that served general interests (railroads, public sector corporations, dams), rather than serving strictly commercial and entrepreneurial interests. In today's process, agrarian social relations in many parts of rural India are being upset, new parties enter local politics, state corruption reaches monumental heights, and agricultural productivity, employment, and livelihood are adversely affected in virtually every state in India. Studies like those by Levien and Cross force us to see that the crisis of the rural and agrarian sector in India is increasingly the product of the vast transfer of agricultural lands to urban commercial interests, with a brokerage fee charge for this service by the Indian state.

Balakrishnan's book, *Shareholder Cities: Land Transformations along Urban Corridors in India* (2019) is directly relevant to my concerns, since it deals with the exact subregion of Maharashtra in which Vadi is located, with Pune and Mumbai as its two major urban centers. What Balakrishnan analyzes, with meticulous documentary and ethnographic research, is the way in which urban industrial formations are being actively sponsored by agrarian elites, who collude with the state to turn major tracts of cheaply acquired agrarian land into capitalist assets, including elite residential complexes. Part of this process involves the replacement of fertility by location in determining price, the transformation of former sugarcane-growing elites into corporate urban shareholders, and the forging of precarious alliances between wealthy and poor castes to maximize the benefits of corporatized urbanism in rural areas. Balakrishnan's story spans some two decades bringing us to about 2015 (from 1996), so as to provide the perfect macro backdrop to what has happened (and what did not happen) in Vadi.

Agricultural Reason

The key term in my title for this collection is "Agricultural Reason." I use this term to capture the fact that farmers in India operate with their own form of "reason," by which I mean that they have clear ideas about means and ends, causes and effects, certainties and likelihoods. In this sense, agricultural reason is like all reason and expresses itself in rules and tools of thought, of varying styles and expressions, whose shared purpose is to allow human beings to get from today to tomorrow. One prejudice of the 1970s, epitomized in Marshall Sahlins's *Culture and Practical Reason* (1976), was to overstate the difference between cultural and practical dispositions, and to treat all of the forms of calculative and instrumental behavior as confined to a bourgeois capitalist worldview, and to see the rest of the world as being solely about the self-reproduction of local cosmologies. This radical culturalism had a repressive effect on much economic anthropology, which was banished to the outhouse of "formalism," though Sahlins was right to speak forcefully about the special characteristics of bourgeois capitalist reason and its echoes in American behavioral science. When I use the term "agricultural reason," I use it to capture those forms of reason which have a universal character in the agentive pursuit of publicly recognized goods but take the form of highly distinctive cultural logics, languages, and beliefs. I am among those who are committed to the idea that no human society or cosmology is irrational, primitive, or savage, as are the majority of my anthropological colleagues.

My interest in "agricultural reason" is that, as a calculative mode which is culturally embedded and articulated, it is still barely visible in studies of Indian villages, regardless of discipline (Gupta 1998 is a noteworthy exception). There have been many rich studies of Indian peasant life, agricultural power systems, and systems of tenancy, debt, and dependency (Bliss and Stern 1982; J. Harriss 1982; Rudra and Bardhan 1983; B. Harriss 1984;) and a vast historical literature on land tenure, revenue farming, and agricultural markets. But attention to how farmers speak, think, and conceptualize their practices and calculations *in their own terms* is notably rare. This aspect of my concerns is the main justification for republishing these essays together and now.

This interest is also what makes this book especially appropriate for HAU Books, with its commitment to "ethnographic theory." The latter term, theory, could be parsed in several ways. One is that the granular details of any way of life are always sediments of a cosmology or worldview which has a theoretical spirit. Another parsing flows from the idea that no ethnography appears written on a tabula rasa, but comes from ideas, questions, and puzzles that the ethnographer brings to her fieldwork from her training, readings, and influences in the broader field of anthropological theory. My own parsing of "ethnographic theory" is that it should also include ethnographies *of* theory, of the nature of concepts, categories, and rationalities embedded in everyday speech and action in every society. This meaning of ethnographic theory encompasses scholars as diverse as Marcel Mauss ([1925] 1954), E. E. Evans-Pritchard (1937), Clifford Geertz (1973), Pierre Bourdieu (1977), and Philippe Descola (2013).

The Biography of the Project

The fieldwork on which this book is based was conducted in 1981–82, almost exactly four decades ago. It grew out of my awareness, as a young assistant professor of anthropology teaching courses about Indian society and culture, that my experience of India was almost entirely urban. Villages and farmers composed the vast bulk of India's physical and demographic landscape, but my knowledge of them was almost entirely mediated by books, and by a few isolated travel experiences outside urban India. My doctoral fieldwork had been in Madras (now Chennai), a large city, a little less cosmopolitan and modern than my hometown, Bombay (now Mumbai).

As a consequence, I was motivated to explore the possibility of doing some serious work on rural India, but on what subject? The study of caste systems, ideologies, and patterns had dominated anthropology for at least three decades. Giant thinkers like McKim Marriott (1955), M. N. Srinivas (1959, 1976), Louis Dumont (1970), and dozens of others seem to have said everything there was to say about how caste works, why it persists, how it shapes Indian economy, society and ritual, and how it changes, or does not. There were whole floors of libraries filled with books on caste. What could I hope to add?

I found a path in the most obvious possibility, which had not attracted much anthropological interest until the late 1970s (nor has it since then). How about an ethnography of agriculture? There were a few distinguished precedents. In his brilliant work on agricultural involution in Indonesia (1963), Clifford Geertz had shown that there was a way to bring cultural, social, and historical analysis to bear on an agrarian system that had grown both intricate and rigid, as an adaptation to the coercive and extractive pressures of the Dutch colonial state. At the same time, a leading Indian sociologist and anthropologist, André Beteille, wrote an important book on agriculture in India and its social framework (1974), thus joining a small group of sociologists of India, including S. J. Tambiah (1958), Joan Mencher (1974), M. N. Srinivas (1976), and Kathleen Gough (1981), who had looked at agrarian life as an important dimension of South Asian society and history. Geertz and Beteille led me to an interest in farmers and agriculture, but here again the question was what I could do. How could I add to the work by agronomists, rural economists, social historians, and other experts who seem to have covered a lot of topics such as tenancy, livestock, credit, productivity, and labor, the latter in the tradition of the great Russian scholar of peasant society, A. V. Chayanov ([1925] 1986)?

Here some other realizations came to my rescue. The first was my observation that while agrarian society had been studied by a few anthropologists, they were largely oriented to considerations of class, land, and resources and did not show much interest in language, culture, or cosmology. Here was an opportunity for me to contribute something. And my inspiration came from a book that swept me off my feet and has never ceased to affect my thinking over the rest of my life. It was Pierre Bourdieu's *Outline of a Theory of Practice*, which appeared in an English translation in 1977. For me, and many others of my generation, this was a life-changing book in its approach to the linkages between cosmology and calculation in traditional societies, in its attention to the practical reason which allowed cosmologies to be reproduced in a flexible manner, and for its analysis of the complex ways in which *doxa* (opinions and beliefs) take historical and social form. Bourdieu's book was my bible when I eventually started fieldwork in the village I have named Vadi, in the state of Maharashtra, in Western India, in Fall 1981.

One other thought had begun to preoccupy me in the mid-1970s and it was that production had dominated too many accounts of the economy, among historians, sociologists, and economists of rural life, and that consumption had largely been taken to be an irrational or arbitrary phase in the lives of most economies. I had, more or less by accident, read Jean Baudrillard's book, *The Mirror of Production* (1975), and been convinced of his argument that from Marx onwards consumption had not been given its full and independent analytic space in the social sciences. I thus saw that consumption could be my gateway into the agrarian world of rural India.

The final piece of the puzzle was to decide how to look at consumption, and in this regard I fell into what later proved to be a cul-de-sac, which was the burgeoning literature of the late 1970s on peasant "decision-making," exemplified by scholars like Sutti Ortiz (1973), Naomi Quinn (1978), and Michael Murtaugh and Hugh Gladwin (1980). Many of these anthropologists were in conversation with psychologists such as Richard E. Nisbett and Lee Ross (1980) and also Daniel Kahneman,

Paul Slovic, and Amos Tversky (1982). Informed by these scholars and by the general field of "culture and cognition," I was awarded a substantial (for the time) grant by the National Science Foundation in 1981, to conduct fieldwork on peasant consumption decisions in Western India. This award began the process which led to the essays reproduced in this volume, all largely written or drafted in the 1980s.

When I first wrote and published these essays, I did not have a clear book project in mind. When I did begin to think of a book built around these essays, I was already in dialogue with economists, statisticians, as well some colleagues in anthropology, about the significance and wider implications of my findings. But it was not clear how to bring them together in a coherent framework which could include influences and interlocutors who differed as widely from one another as Bourdieu (1977) and Geertz (1963) on the one hand, and some economists of agrarian India such as Pranab Bardhan, Ashok Rudra, and T. N. Srinivasan on the other, who thought my work was interesting but somehow not adequately representative or generalizable. While I was in this state of indecision, my interests had begun to shift to the "social life of things" (Appadurai 1986a) and to the study of transnational cultural process, which led to the formation of the journal *Public Culture* in 1988. These interests led me to several subsequent decades of work on globalization, mediation, violence, and related issues which left my essays on agriculture to lead their individual lives in sometimes hard-to-find publications.

These essays tell us, at the simplest level, how small farmers eking out a living on land with scarce water, tiny holdings, and limited labor fashion out a living on the edges of two kinds of subsistence capitalism, a term discussed at the beginning of this introduction. One kind is the capitalism of markets for their commercial cultigens, including onions, sugarcane, chickpeas, green peas, and coriander (cilantro), the last being the most delicate and risky for the farmer. These cultigens command markets in the nearby town of Saswad (about 5 kilometers from Vadi), the bigger city of Pune (about 35 kilometers from Vadi), and the metropolis of Mumbai, (about 180 kilometers from Vadi). These urban markets are, of course, subject to demand and price fluctuations and only a tiny number of big farmers are protected from these fluctuations. For the bulk of the farmers of Vadi and their 170 or so households (out of a total of about 190) in 1981, the sale of these commercial crops allowed them to meet their consumption needs without much profit or savings.

The second feature of subsistence capitalism was the employment of many male farmers in urban settings, such as Mumbai, where many worked in the textile mills, others worked as sugarcane juice vendors, a few as vegetable market middlemen, and in Pune, as auto-rickshaw drivers or in other low-paid professions. These migrant male workers did their best to return to their village at key points in the agrarian calendar, and were able to remit some sums of money to their families, but their main contribution to the subsistence of their families was to relieve them of the daily consumption needs of one or a few family members. Indeed, the term subsistence might be too positive to fit the numbers of small farmers who live under or close to the poverty line.

The shadow of subsistence capitalism, which I invoke in my title, thus has two sources, neither of which benefits small farmers, who can be defined as those who own less than two hectares of land and who were in 1980 and remain today about 80 percent of all farmers. There are about 100 million farmers in India, and thus about 80 million people constitute the larger demographic into which fit the small farmers of Vadi, where households with less than two hectares constituted more than 80 percent of all the households in 1981. Still, the qualitative point here is that the condition of the small farmers whom I worked with in 1981–82 is as dismal, or worse, today than it was then. This is another important justification for presenting these essays based on fieldwork done in 1981–82.

I said above that my interest in formal models of peasant decision-making proved to be a cul-de-sac, which I rapidly abandoned. The main reason for this is that these formal models rely on the capacity of ordinary people to reconstruct their own decisions accurately, without amnesia, bias, or embarrassment. I discovered in the field that no one remembers exactly why they did what they did, and when they do, it is in ways that do not resemble at all the terminology of formal models of decision-making. There may have been formal techniques known to others which could have helped me overcome this obstacle, but I was making enough sense of what I was seeing and hearing with other tools to dispense with these formal models from the cognitive and decision sciences.

There is an important theme which links these essays. Each of them underlines the force of the social, even in the harshest circumstances of inequality, environmental hazard, and family adversity. Whether it is in the sharing of water from the many dug wells in the village, or in the exchange of bullocks during plowing and harvest times, or the transactions in the borrowing and sharing of food in the rituals of domestic hospitality, or in the celebrations of weddings and festivals, the sense of the primacy and value of the social in all efforts to subsist is a discernable feature of the workings of agricultural reason. This stubborn sociality is the main bulwark of these poor farmers living in the shadow of subsistence capitalism. I will return to the themes of sociality and the social in the conclusion to this introduction.

Chapter 1, titled "*Andāj*" is on the "terminology of measurement," and is the anchor essay for this volume. The word *andāj*, derived from Persian, has a wide range of meanings in Marathi, the predominant language in Maharashtra, but in this context it means "estimate" or "approximate." The essay was written originally after just four months of fieldwork in Vadi. It exemplifies my main argument throughout this set of papers, which is that every part of the social world of Vadi embeds technical forms in cultural styles. This may well be true of many other social worlds far from Maharashtra in 1981. In this essay, I outline in some detail the ways in which measurement in Vadi relies on approximation rather than precision, and almost all measures are subject to negotiations. Further, I observe that measures and standards are often metonyms for one another, and these measures and standards produce algorithms for agrarian practice that can range from tautologies to estimates derived from historical contexts. The importance of this chapter is both conceptual and methodological. Its conceptual importance is that it offers a significant corrective to our notion that true measurement is precise, context-free, and universal. But that view is *our* ideology of measurement, a product of the Western seventeenth century, grounded in the scientific revolution but gradually transformed into a general worldview. Much of the rest of the world thinks about measurement differently, as an algorithmic tool for socially credible estimation. Vadi is an example of this latter form of reasoning, whose embeddedness is an epistemological quality and not a sign of mental fuzziness or disinterest in truth. It undergirds many other aspects of life in Vadi, as can be seen in the other chapters collected here. The methodological significance of the arguments of this chapter is that, as social scientists, we need to be careful about treating our own ideologies of measurement as metasystems, which can contain and translate other ideologies. Such humility should extend to our ideas of inequality, poverty, and class, which are all expressions of particular ideologies of distance, difference, and domination.

The chapter that follows, on problems of scale, chapter 2, shifts the measurement problem to a methodological terrain, and explores how I faced the challenge of linking what I call relational and distributional dimensions of rural life in Vadi. This exploration leads me to various suggestions about linking the micro work of ethnography to the macro concerns of economists and statisticians. The key conceptual distinction in this essay is between what I call "distributional" and "relational" measures. The former type of measure is best suited to large-scale, aggregative, and sampling methods, since they are about quantities of various kinds of assets and groups. The latter type is best suited to ethnographic, interpretive, and cultural methods, since they are about qualities, relations, and social meanings. In this chapter, I explore some ways to commensurate and coordinate these methods. Alas, the dialogue between statisticians and ethnographers has not advanced very much since I first wrote this essay, possibly because neither discipline exposes its students to the other one. It is also possible that the arrival of pattern-seeking in big data, remote sensing, and other digital methods has offered different options for the study of issues of aggregation and of the relationship between scales.

Chapter 3 homes in on a very specific technology, that of open-surface wells and their intricate, culturally marked capacity to create access to water for poor farmers who must share water or lose their small capacity to subsist in a dry agricultural area. This chapter is based on what I later realized is an example of the "agricultural involution" Geertz (1963) astutely wrote about in Java, mentioned above, to refer to the way in which intensive rice cultivation under Dutch rule created the immense overexploitation by a growing population of a limited supply of new land. In turn this drove ecological and economic "involution," namely, more people producing fewer agricultural goods. In Vadi, the complex and fragmented nature of "shares" in well water makes cooperation among villagers, especially agnates, workable but not necessarily desirable, since autonomy was evidently the biggest desire of the majority of farmers. Wells in Vadi are thus a lens into the ambivalences surrounding cooperation in the shadow of subsistence capitalism. The close study of wells in regions like Maharashtra is especially important because it reveals the opposing pulls of competition and cooperation in the context of subsistence capitalism. If a small farmer does not want the complexities of these pulls for a tiny share in the water from a shared well, his only choice would be to stay outside the world of commercial crops and survive only on crops for family consumption, thus pushing the family closer to the edge of bare subsistence and/or cash debt.

Chapter 4 looks at cooperation and sharing in the context of food and domestic sociality to show how improvisation of the most creative sort, especially by women, is a critical condition and lubricant of everyday sociality in Vadi. Here I take a close look at the multiple roles of women in the families of smallholders and pay close attention to the relationships between gender, consumption, and production. Women are often misrepresented as icons of habitus in many such worlds. In truth, they are masters of improvisation, as they deal with difficult husbands, seasonal volatilities in the fields and in the market, ups and downs in the demand for their own labor, the burdens of the care-taking of elders, children, and domestic animals. All this is done in the context of the special role of women in all the rituals of the agrarian religious calendar, which is intimately intercalibrated with the ecological calendar. When they spoke to me and to one another, women were eloquent about how difficult their lives were prone to be. Diet is a meeting point of improvisations in the reproduction of everyday life in which women bear a disproportionate and difficult share. Except for the heavy work of plowing, there is not much that the women of Vadi do not do, and much of it is to provide support to their male family members in every aspect of agrarian life.

Finally, in Chapter 5, I deepen the analysis of the relationship between technological change and the domain of values, by returning to wells, commercialization, cooperation, and the sociality of subsistence in Vadi. The argument here is an effort to find a third way, which might be superior to a radical cultural protectionism of lifeworlds such as those of Vadi as well as preferable to those economistic valuations of externally induced challenge, which prioritize recent forms of individualism, maximization, and marketized thought. This third way can be found in the prime value of sociality, which is here seen as a highly particular form of the Aristotelian or Durkheimian valuation of the social. The prime or core value of sociality is sufficiently central to the meaningful order of life in Vadi as to be a strong candidate to serve as a metric to resolve debates about defensible—as opposed to indefensible—forms of technical change. The inroads of commercialization affect the cost of water, fertilizer, and labor and the social costs for marriages, funerals, and hosting. But they also materially transform the nature of sociality, as I shall argue in the next and final section.

A Coda on the Social and on Sociality

I have said very little in this introduction about caste, partly because the Maratha caste, though internally stratified, constituted more than ninety percent of the population of Vadi. Yet, caste is always a crucial part of life in every part of India, including Maharashtra, and has been studied closely for the better part of the past century (among the landmarks of this tradition that focus on Maharashtra are: Karve 1968; Carter 1974; Schlesinger 1981; Attwood 1992; Baviskar and Attwood 1995; Omvedt 1995).

Maharashtra is also the home state of the great Dalit constitutionalist, B. R. Ambedkar, and is one of the major regions in which Untouchables, inspired by Ambedkar, converted to Buddhism and exited Brahmanical Hinduism. At the same time, Maharashtra is a major part of the history of Brahman domination in state politics (going back to the Maratha period) and Pune and Nagpur, among other cities, have been hotbeds of right-wing Hinduism for decades. But over the last few centuries, members of the Maratha population grew to be almost thirty-three percent of the population of the state, and were the unquestionable "dominant caste" (Srinivas 1959) of this region. It could be argued that mobility, inequality, and internal solidarity *among* Marathas is much more important than their relationship either to Brahmans or to Untouchable castes, especially since Indian independence.

In retrospect, I regret that my youth, lack of exposure to Dalit life and politics, and my urban, upper-caste biography kept me away from a deeper engagement with the Dalit settlements and families of Vadi. I do know that they were silent, segregated, and largely invisible, both to me and to the bulk of the upper castes. My Maratha interlocutors, teachers, and friends in Vadi also insulated me from the Dalit world. Still, many dimensions of rural poverty, inequality, and ontology were highly articulated *within* the relations of the 160 or so Maratha households of Vadi in the early 1980s. I have also become convinced that most interpretations of rural power dynamics in India have been distorted. On the one hand, many Marxist or semi-Marxist interpretations of rural inequality fail to fit the square peg of unequal material assets into the round hole of purity, pollution, and social segregation which define caste ideology. On the other hand, many culturalist explanations of rural inequality and power relations simply subordinate economic stratification to ritual and cosmological grammars, without accounting for their potency or persistence. The middle path is filled by dozens of empirical studies which simply refuse to connect these factors, and remain content to catalog their adjacency.

I have placed much emphasis, in the five following chapters in this collection, on sociality as the core value which is sustained by Vadi's farmers in the face of the depredations of subsistence capitalism. Whether in the sharing of bullocks, in the improvisations of diet and hospitality, in the intricate sharing of wells and irrigation technologies, or in the use of measures which have no interest in transcending social negotiation, the farmers of Vadi treat sociality as both their primary interest and their primary asset.

In using the term "sociality" I do *not* mean to imply that Vadi is a cozy gemeinschaft of equals, a romantic volk community. It is not. I mean by sociality something more like "relationality," which no one in Vadi can do without. And relationality here does *not* mean symmetry, though it does mean reciprocity. But reciprocity is not a relationship between equals, as a century of studies of village caste systems have shown. This set of distinctions, between sociality, relationality, and reciprocity, may have relevance to other peasant societies, but it is especially relevant to India, where caste has been an axiological principle for almost two millennia. Yet, how caste works and what it means remain topics of deep debate.

In a micro-community like Vadi, though it does not have the steep and pervasive verticality of other Indian village communities, due to the demographic domination of the Maratha caste and the scarcity of an agrarian surplus in a semi-arid region, it is nevertheless not possible to understand its social life outside those rules of purity, status, marriage, and kinship which define caste society. So, the large question with which I will end this coda, and this introductory essay, is about how caste as a lived ideology affects rural inequality in India. The list of distinguished scholars who have addressed this question is too long for individual attribution, and I have already touched on some of its leading figures. But in light of the central subject of this book, which is agriculture, I offer the following reflection.

Agriculture as a form of livelihood in India as a whole is the critical material reality which mediates caste and sociality. I repeat now that for me sociality is about relationality, with no necessary implications for equality or mutuality. Relationality in Indian rural settings, especially under the conditions of subsistence capitalism, holds different groups together, even when considerations of purity and pollution might pull them apart. Because of the special scarcity of the key means of production—land, water, cattle, and labor—relationality is both asymmetrical and compulsory. In this sense, agriculture provides the centripetal pull against the centrifugal pull of caste. Their mutual tension is the governing logic of the agrarian habitus in India.

This agricultural relationality, as I try to show in the detailed essays about Vadi, is the counterpoint to the inner logic of caste, which is about difference, repulsion, and distance as its primary logic, a logic identified as early as the ground-breaking work of the French scholar Célestin Bouglé ([1908] 1971). From this point of view, it is true that there is a complex material reality, the reality of agricultural relationality, which allows the caste system to reproduce itself over centuries in spite of its abhorrence of any sort of contact between castes. Yet this material reality cannot be reduced entirely to the means of production because it is embedded in an ontology which is fully and irreducibly cultural, and composed of words and concepts which are deeply local.

Thus, when I argue that sociality is the core value which accounts for key aspects of the habitus of Vadi, I intend to point to the logic which connects subsistence agriculture to a wider Indian world of inequality, inequity, and poverty. But agriculture cannot be reduced to its technical dimensions. It is itself immersed in a form of reason that is inescapably cultural. In this sense, the primary aim of this collection of essays is to demonstrate the ways in which an agrarian world can be a fully cultural expression, while also being poor, unequal, and peripheral.

CHAPTER I

Andāj

The Problem[1]

Rural terminologies for measurement, and the ideas and epistemological strategies they embody, present several problems that make them worth investigating. First, they differ radically from contemporary Western, scientific systems in their assumptions and in their popular expressions. Contemporary Western systems regard measurement as a distinct technical activity, subject to rigid and relatively abstract standards; in turn, these standards (as concepts) are sharply distinguished from the instruments of measurement; further, such instruments are clearly separated from the objects or phenomena they are intended to measure. Measurement in the contemporary West, therefore, is regarded as a precise technical activity, theoretically free of social, moral, or cultural coloration, a value-free descriptive activity. This state of affairs, of course, reflects a long and complex historical process, whereby scientific conceptions come to dominate more practical and cosmological ones, and technical

---

1. This essay is based on fieldwork done in 1981–82 in rural Maharashtra. I have changed as little as possible of the tone and tense, since it is my view that the terms and concepts of agricultural measurement do not change much in short periods of time. Still, this essay should be read as an effort to capture a rural epistemology at a specific moment in time in order to open a discussion about the durability of such an epistemology and how it might change over time.

progress both encourages and expresses this tendency. It is, of course, outside the scope of this chapter to explore this Western story, but its implications are reasonably clear.[2]

In rural India, by contrast (as in many agricultural communities in the world), the terminology of measurement reflects a radically different universe of meanings and practices. The activity of measurement is interwoven with other modes of evaluation and description. Its terminology does not recognize the boundary between technical, ritual, and everyday activity. The standards embodied in the terminology are frequently simply labels for the instruments of measurement. The instruments are often themselves standardized descriptions of the phenomena or objects themselves. By extension, measurement in such contexts is neither precise nor value-free, but is shot through with the signs of local variation, cosmological symbolism, and the vagueness and approximateness which characterizes ordinary life. The language of measurement is, therefore, not the "cool" language of technical description and comparison but the "hot" language of judgment and evaluation, embedded in particular social contexts and signifying larger cultural and cosmological understandings.

These contrasts, which constitute a significant problem of cross-cultural analysis in their own right, lead to the second problem posed by rural Indian terminologies of measurement, and this is a problem of method for those social scientists concerned with understanding rural life in general, and its agricultural framework in particular. Economists and sociologists (both Indian and Western) come to rural communities armed with just those assumptions, instruments, and techniques of measurement which are most alien to the indigenous ethos of measurement. This is, of course, especially true of large, quantitatively oriented, survey-based studies concerned with "aggregate" patterns of behavior. It

---

2. Since this chapter does not have elaborate notes, let me note here some prior work that has been extremely influential in the formulation of the ideas contained in it. In regard to the general approach to the analysis of cultural systems, I owe a great deal to the many writings of Clifford Geertz, in particular an essay called "Common Sense as a Cultural System" (1975). Equally influential, especially in regard to the cultural ethos of peasantry, has been *Outline of a Theory of Practice* by Pierre Bourdieu (1977) and, by the same author, "The Attitude of the Algerian Peasant Toward Time" (1963). I have also benefited by a great deal of work by agroeconomists working in India. In particular, I have derived much benefit from the prolific writings of Narpat S. Jodha on the agricultural economics of the semi-arid tropics (for one example see, Jodha 1992).

is equally true of agronomic and economic studies which, even when they are small-scale, contain the same assumptions. The terminological, cultural, and rhetorical clash this encounter must provoke is rarely acknowledged, much less diagnosed or interpreted. Anthropologists, who might be expected to be more forthright in addressing the problem, given their more holistic, "humanistic," local, and cultural orientation, have also largely avoided the problem, possibly because they have often ignored or underplayed the practical/agricultural aspects of rural life altogether. Historians of rural India have generally not done better, but in their case, they are coping with the double refraction of records that frequently themselves are the product of external and extra-local processes of translation, distortion, and political standardization. There is, therefore, some methodological urgency in trying to describe and interpret rural and local systems of measurement, as far as possible, in their own terms, before leaping in with clocks and censuses, surveys and tape measures, rain gauges, and aerial photographs, all of which are a cultural world apart from the human beings they seek to "measure." The implications of such caution for research oriented toward agricultural development should need no elaboration. Neither the purposes of scholarship nor those of directed social change are served by ignoring this particular terminological chasm.

The third problem posed by rural terminologies of measurement concerns the contrast between regional and civilizational modes of discourse, within India. As in other kinds of terminology, the language of measurement remains highly localized, idiosyncratic, historically conservative, and relatively intractable to external efforts at standardization. Until the period of colonial rule, rural systems of measurement (whether of land, money, or taxation) remained highly fragmented. Colonial rule, and its post-independence successor, can be read in part as being involved in an uphill battle to subordinate such variation to national (and international) standards. This process continues today and is dealt with toward the end of this chapter. Of course, long before colonial rule, certain Hindu civilizational standards had clearly penetrated rural terminologies. An excellent case is that of the Hindu calendar which today, in some form, affects the rural perception and organization of time. But, as we shall see, this pan-Indian terminology plays a very uneven and sometimes secondary role in rural discourse involving measurement.

To the extent that the indigenous textual tradition contains information relevant to rural modes of measurement, this might be worthy of more systematic investigation, but, in general, these texts are likely to contain a variety of culturally and historically generated standards (how many days should a Brahmana observe death pollution? What is the duration of a *nakshatra*? What portion of the yield of the land is the king's share? etc.), rather than revealing the nature of rural systems of measurement, seen as examples of language in use.[3] For, as I hope to show, measurement in rural India is above all a practical activity, rooted in a complex cosmology, but oriented to solving the myriad problems of daily rural life. In this sense, it is likely that all these local systems in India share a good many features (as perhaps do all premodern agricultural systems) but what they share is unlikely to be, except in a superficial sense, a common Hindu terminology. It is also possible to make the case that rural Indian systems of measurement, rooted as they are in agricultural activity, constitute an especially interesting topic of study, because of the relative paucity of premodern texts dealing directly with agriculture. In any case, they constitute an excellent entry into the mentality and ways of knowing of rural folk in India, and a crucial point of contact between peasant discourse and agricultural practice.

If the data contained in this chapter are even reasonably persuasive, they should also make a strong methodological argument: namely, that rural concepts of measurement require not simply to be glossed with their nearest Western equivalents but, like other cultural phenomena, to be interpreted in context. This is what, at least in a preliminary way, I expect to achieve in the remainder of this chapter.

The Ethnographic Context

The descriptive examples in this chapter are the product of a research project conducted in 1981–82 on culture and consumption in a rural community in Maharashtra, here referred to by the pseudonym Vadi (Appadurai 1984c, 1989a, 1990, 1991).[4] Vadi is a village in Western

---

3. Although a detailed discussion of the ancient roots of current rural systems of measurement is outside the scope of this paper, mention should be made of a first-class book by Saradha Srinivasan, *Mensuration in Ancient India* (1979). This study provides a superb overview of the textual as well as the inscriptional material relevant to ancient Indian measurement, and, amongst other things, indicates the rural and practical origin of many classical terms of measure.

4. These publications are included in this volume as chapters 2–5.

Maharashtra in the Purandhar taluka of Pune District. It lies in the mixed ecological zone where the eastern slopes of the Sahyadri mountains (the Western Ghats) give way to the semi-arid drought-prone area of the Deccan Plateau. It is approximately 40 kilometers southeast of Pune and about 6 kilometers from the market town and *taluq* headquarters of Saswad. The village consists of approximately 200 hearths,[5] distributed socially and spatially in a bewildering combination of family types and dwellings. About 75 percent of these families reside in the village proper, while the rest live in about seven clusters of dwellings in the surrounding fields.

Agriculture is virtually the sole means of livelihood in the village, although many households have at least one person working in Pune or Mumbai. Land is scarce, and the large majority of farmers own less than 5 acres of land. Irrigated land is less than 25 percent of the total, and comes mostly from wells powered by electric pumps. Dependence on rainfall is very high, and the average annual precipitation is no greater than 625 millimeters (25 inches). *Jowar* (sorghum) and *bajri* (pearl millet) are the main crops, and also form the staples of the local diet. Also grown, however, are modest amounts of sugarcane, rice, wheat, pulses, onions, coriander, and a large number of other vegetables. Of the large number of vegetables grown, onions and coriander are grown principally for sale and the remainder are intended primarily for home consumption. Many adult men and women work as agricultural laborers in the villages surrounding Vadi and in Vadi itself, in addition to working their own minuscule plots. The large number of villagers engaged in salaried jobs in Pune and Mumbai is regarded as the product of land scarcity and labor surplus in Vadi, and as a device to smooth out the unpredictable, and often inadequate yields of local holdings.

The village is dominated by the ideology of subsistence, which may be defined as characterized by a constant fear that income from agriculture will fall short of household consumption needs. Even the big farmers (i.e., those with more than 10 acres of land) share this ideology, although they are in transparently better economic shape than their poorer neighbors. Almost 95 percent of the families in Vadi belong to the Maratha caste and these are largely divided into five out-marrying patrilineages. There are no more than fifteen households belonging to other castes, the bulk of these belonging to what were traditionally regarded

---

5. The facts and figures in the following paragraph are tentative, since the results of a survey conducted by the author are still not fully analyzed.

as "untouchable" categories. This gives the village a considerable feeling of social homogeneity which is deepened by the shared subsistence predicament of the majority of families. In an environment characterized by low capital, low and uncertain rainfall, largely unirrigated land, relatively poor soil, tiny holdings, and uncertain cash income from urban employment and local agricultural labor, it is no surprise that men and women in Vadi are deeply preoccupied with the struggle to make ends meet. These struggles result in constant, though perhaps often unspoken, calculation. Such calculation, however, rarely conforms to formal models of planning, choice, estimation of probabilities, scanning of alternatives, or entrepreneurial risk-taking. In what then does it consist? The beginning of an answer to this gigantic question lies in close inspection of local models of measurement, which both underline and symbolize key aspects of this very particular brand of calculation.

The Practical Ethos of Peasant Measurement

The general ethos of peasant measurement can best be grasped by noticing its intimate relationship to a host of practical considerations. Far from representing a technical system externally applied to specific situations, its conceptions and terms are frequently simply historically formed and culturally derived metaphors for these situations. Thus, there are a few abstract and general standards but rather a host of specific terminologies appropriate to different classes of phenomena. Take the terminology of time, for example: major agricultural moments and key seasonal transitions are referred to in the idiom of the Hindu calendar, and oriented by the complex system of lunar months, *nakshatras*, and *tithis* (dates) contained in a regional *panchānga* (almanac). But the key activities of agricultural production (sowing, harvesting, plowing, etc.) are temporarily demarcated by the gross binary contrast between the *kharif* and *rabi* growing seasons (fall harvest and spring harvest growing seasons, roughly June–September and October–February). Yet other issues related to the erratic supply of water, the variable pressure on farmers' time, and the climatic context of agriculture are discussed in terms of the tripartite division of the year into a wet (*pāvsālā*), cold (*hivālā*), and hot (*unhālā*) season. The term *hangām* (season) is applied to both the dual and tripartite classifications. Very complex events are often discussed in terms that conflate each of these systems: thus, a marriage may be recollected as having taken place in a certain *nakshatra*, in the hot season, just before the *kharif* sowing of sorghum. The same high degree of specificity applies to the measurement of different crop yields: while the yield of basic grains is measured in *poti* (a large fiber bag), the yield of onions is measured in bags of different sizes and with another name (*pishvī*), the yield of coriander (*kothimbīr*) is measured in *khurāda* (a small basket), and of sugarcane in truckloads. Traditional wells are often measured by the number of oxen required to raise the steel containers containing their water, by the number of months during which they yield water, or by the number of farmers who share their water.

It follows from this practical proliferation of terminologies that the standards of measurement are frequently themselves labels for the instruments of measurement. Thus, as in the previous example, the yields of grain and vegetables are frequently measured by standards (bags, bunches, truckloads, cartloads, etc.) which are identical with the instruments of measurement themselves. Perhaps the best examples of this conflation of standards and instruments can be seen in the use of the human body for measurement. For agricultural activities that involve the measurement of small lengths, a measure called the *pānd* is used which refers to an adult's normal pace length. Thus, the width of one farmer's plot which is otherwise undivided from his neighbor's plot is frequently measured in *pānd*; similarly, a farmer may speak of planting 13 *pānd* of coriander (although he will measure the yield in the baskets used for collecting the coriander harvest). In a situation where plot sizes are frequently extremely small, (less than half an acre) and where cropping patterns are extremely involute, the practical function of this measure is obvious.

In domestic or ritual contexts, especially involving informal and small-scale transactions in grain, salt, sugar, flour, or other dry food items, villagers speak of fist-full (*mūth-bhar*) or of a *vanjala* (a measure referring to the full capacity of the two open palms held contiguously). In the planting of onions for the growing of onion seeds the distance between the plants is measured in hand-spans (*vīt*) and in the planting of garlic the cloves are spaced three finger-lengths (*bota: tin botāche antarane*). In a looser and more metaphoric way, meals are often judged as being stomach-filling (*pot-bhar*) or not, and in estimating the labor requirements of key agricultural tasks (such as plowing or sowing), complex multivariate standards are referred to which include the variables of number of men ("bodies"), bullocks, and working days.

Just as the standards of measurement are not abstractions distinct from the instruments used in their application (as a mile is distinct from the milestones that embody its extent, and the hour from the hands and the face of the clock that measure its passage), so also the instruments of measurement are often simply standardized forms or metonyms of the objects or phenomena they are used to measure. Thus, distances are frequently measured by reference to the shared practical knowledge of fixed points in the natural or man-made landscape and the duration is frequently measured by reference to collectively recalled events in the past or expected events in the future. This can frequently be frustrating for the investigator who seeks an independent (i.e., abstract) measure of time or space and who, in the absence of the shared and tacit experience and knowledge which makes such measures meaningful, responds to them as tautologies which in a certain logical sense they are. (For example: Question: How far is your family's well from the village? Answer: Just on the other side of the river [*nadīchyā palīkade*]; or Question: When did you buy your bullocks? Answer: Just before I planted my *kharif bajri* last year [*kharīf bājrī pernīchā agodar*]). Examples of the metonymic relationship between instrument of measurement and object to be measured also abound: garlic yields are often measured in bunches (*pend*), rainfall by the degree of runoff in fields, tasks by the amount of men and bullocks and days required to complete them (rather than by such abstractions as man-hours). The extreme examples of such tautological propositions are when, for example, a farmer is asked what his sorghum yield was last season, and he replies that it was just enough for his family's consumption needs (*gharchyā khānyāsāthi parvadla*); or when asked for how many days he has to rent bullocks for the *kharif* sowing of *jowar*, he replies that he rents them for as long as it takes to complete the job. Such tautological statements are entirely uninformative to the outside investigator precisely because their experiential and tacit context is not well understood by villagers. The give and take between villagers on matters of measurement, frequently, has this tautological and uninformative quality. In a negative sense, these features of the rural mode of measurement (i.e., the thin line between the standards and the instruments of measurement and the equally thin line between the instruments and the objects/phenomena to be measured) are the product of the lack of precise technologies. But in a positive sense, they result from the fact that the language of measurement is a part and parcel of the practical contexts that have generated it. This context sensitivity of measurement does not imply that the bewildering array of standards and measures is an atomized and incoherent aggregate. Indeed, the opposite is the case, and in a later section of this chapter, I will address the relationship between standards and measures.

The observation that rural terminologies of measurement refer to standards, instruments, and measures that are intimately, indissolubly, and intricately rooted in practical contexts immediately directs our attention to the culturally and historically shaped environment in which such terminologies function. The practical wisdom of farmers (of which terminologies of measurement are an essential part) is geared to coping with certain attributes of their environment. This is not, however, to suggest that rural modes of measurement are in any simple way determined by ecological or technological factors. Rather the accumulated cultural and historical experience of a certain set of ecological, technological, and social factors is expressed in the terminology of measurement. The environment of Vadi is characterized by high degrees of variability, uncertainty, and fluctuation in regard to the key phenomena.

Variability characterizes every key feature of the human and natural environment of Vadi. The types of land (both in external agronomic categories as well as in local categories) belonging to the farmers of Vadi vary considerably in terms of depth, moisture retentiveness, stoniness, slope, and other factors of which local farmers are aware. A few farmers possess contiguous plots with uniform soil properties, and further, these small and fragmented holdings vary in terms of their access to water, their distance from the farmer's home, their exposure to the dangers of grazing animals, and their vulnerability to crop theft. This social and ecological variability both causes and complicates the extremely convoluted cropping patterns of individual farmers. These cropping-patterns are, in part, efforts to compensate for the variability of their plots, and what they imply is another level of variability in terms of what farmers feel they have to do from day to day, from week to week, from month to month, from season to season, and from year to year. The temporal dimension of variability is uncertainty and this is above all perceived as the central problem regarding rainfall, in Vadi as in other villages in arid and semi-arid regions. Indeed, coping with the uncertainty of rainfall, in villages such as Vadi, may be regarded as the most continuous and conspicuous preoccupation of farmers: predicting the rainfall, organizing agricultural activities around the fact or expectation of rain, husbanding and allocating rainwater, etc. But rainfall is not the only source of uncertainty: plant disease, labor availability (both for buyers and sellers of labor), and crop yields are equally perceived as uncertain.

The most frequent quantitative consequence of the variability and uncertainty of the rural world of Vadi is fluctuation: in crop yields, in prices for commodities (both bought and sold, both agricultural and household), in supplies of essential goods (like fertilizers, diesel fuel, and even electricity), in supplies of essential services (like those of laborers or of other specialists). These kinds of variability, uncertainty, and fluctuation permeate the lives of farmers in Vadi. Terminologies of measurement in an environment of this sort are rooted in practice in a double sense. On the one hand, their extreme specificity and context-rootedness reflect the material conditions of this environment. On the other hand, such terminologies reflect the culturally organized struggle to live tolerable lives, and eke out tolerable livelihoods against the rhythms of such variability, fluctuation, and uncertainty. From this predicament flows a language of measurement, which is intimately linked to the tasks of ordinary life. But ordinary life, in a village like Vadi, is hardly smooth, regular, or free of surprise. Rural terminologies of measurement, therefore, take on a number of other interrelated properties which are explored in each of the following sections of this chapter.

Measurement as Approximation

Contemporary, scientific modes of measurement may be said to be predicated on the assumption that to be accurate is to be precise. In such rural worlds as that of Vadi, it may well be argued that to be accurate is to be approximate. This feature of peasant discourse involving measurement is in fact, once properly understood, less paradoxical than it seems. At any rate, approximation is the most obvious, ubiquitous, and inescapable feature of peasant discourse about their livelihoods. Its concealment is the single largest methodological weakness of those disciplines that seek to analyze rural life in general and agriculture in particular.

Once recognized, it appears in the form of the following contradiction, which ought to be familiar to anyone who has attempted to study rural life at first hand. On the one hand, most farmers in rural areas impress outside investigators as knowledgeable, thoughtful, and reflective about their own lives and about their agricultural problems. They appear to be constantly weighing their needs, scrutinizing their resources, marshaling their capabilities, and evaluating their prospects. In relation to each of these activities, they strike the observer as being shrewd, calculative, and practical in very specific ways. On the other hand, these very farmers are frequently irritatingly vague in their answers to questions about yields, costs, dates, numbers, and virtually anything else that the investigator wishes to measure precisely. Their replies are often reluctant, their estimates shift even in the course of a single conversation; frequently, they simply do not seem to possess the answers to questions that appear very salient to their lives.

Most agricultural researchers bulldoze their way through this embarrassing contradiction in a variety of ways. The ambiguity, vagueness, and elasticity of a farmer's responses are frequently put down to a variety of factors such as their lack of literacy, their suspiciousness of the motives of the investigators, their lack of precise recording and measuring devices, and the like. These explanations may have something to do with the frustrating imprecision of farmers' discourse about the measurable aspects of their lives, but what I would like to suggest is that such imprecision is indeed part of the calculative wisdom of such farmers, and is part of a terminology of measurement that reflects the conditions in which they function and the kind of flexibility that is most appropriate to the analysis of these conditions.

In my own experience in Vadi, both in conversations with me and in conversations at which I was present, I have almost never witnessed a specific quantitative question which has been answered with a single number or figure. Whether the issue involves time, distance, prices, costs, yields, or human or cattle or electric-pump counts, the reply is almost always given in terms of what may be described as the hyphenated measure—i.e., a response which involves two numbers or quantities as if they were a single quantitative evaluation. Examples of such hyphenation are limitless, and exceptions are few and striking. Ask a farmer how many acres of land he owns and he is likely to reply: 7–8 (*sat-āth*) acres; ask him when he is going to harvest his onions and the reply may well be that he will do so in 6–7 (*sahā-sāt*) days. Ask him how often his onions have to be watered and he might say 12–15 times. When one farmer asks another when next he is going to Pune, he is likely to reply that he will do so in 2–4 weeks, or when one villager tells another when they will meet to discuss a matter of mutual interest, he might suggest 3–4 p.m. (*tīn-chār vājtā*). Ask a villager about the cost of fertilizer for his coriander crop and he is likely to report that it was 50–60 rupees. Ask him how many women he employed last year to harvest his onions and a typical reply would be 8–10.

It would be easy to attribute such hyphenated terminology to various disabilities of farmers like illiteracy, poor memory, bad records, poor instruments, and downright mental laziness. In some cases, these charges may well have some basis. What I would like to suggest, however, is that this hyphenated terminology, especially for numerical measurement, is directly related to the variability, uncertainty, and fluctuation that characterized their condition, and which I discussed in the previous section on the ethos of measurement. For every hyphenated measure cited in the previous paragraph, it is possible to make the case that the underlying problem is one of these three features of their situation. However much a farmer may wish to be sure when in the coming week he is going to harvest his onions, the coordination of labor, with his own other commitments, and with weather conditions, makes it ridiculous to be committed to a specific day, even within a short foreseeable future. How often he waters his onions depends on the precise frequency of rainfall during the growing season (which is uncertain), the plot on which he is obliged to grow them, the functioning of the electric pump of the well in which he has a time-share (*pāli*), and so on. His plans to go to Pune are constrained by such a large variety of contingent circumstances that only a loose plan makes sense. As for prices, whether of fertilizer, labor, or other goods, these fluctuate sufficiently (from season to season and sometimes from week to week, from job to job, from village to village) that only hyphenated responses are reasonably adequate. Even in the seemingly straightforward case of the amount of land he owns, the farmer has to consider his fallow lands (some of which are permanent fallows and therefore are countable in one sense and discountable in another) and those portions which are taken up by wells, channels, hedges, cattle or human paths, threshing grounds, storage areas for the piles (*buchchād*) of harvested but unthreshed grain, and so forth. In this last case, of course, some farmers do give precise responses based on the amounts to which they hold legal title in the land records, while others give the more accurate hyphenated response.

This phenomenon of hyphenation in indigenous rural terminologies of measurement, then, can be succinctly characterized as a perfectly reasonable, and accurate, tendency to respond to a certain class of quantitative enquiries with ranges rather than absolute unilateral measures. Replies framed in terms of ranges reflect the ongoing effort of farmers to typify experiences of quantity which are frequently characterized by uncertainty and fluctuation and only rarely by certainty and fixity. It must be added that this is not only characteristic of farmers' responses to the quantitative enquiries of the outside observer but is entirely characteristic of their verbal transactions with each other. Needless to say, this aspect of the terminology of measurement causes considerably more frustration to the investigator seeking single and unambiguous responses, than to the actors themselves who share the knowledge and experience of the host of variables that encourage the language of ranges and discourage the language of discrete measures.

Yet even this is a very rough and excessively functionalist account of the role of approximation in the terminology of measurement in Vadi, and the hyphenated measure is only one aspect of the rhetoric of approximation. The statements in which such hyphenated measures occur, when closely examined, reveal that farmers, in making estimates of quantity, do not typically distinguish what, from the external point of view, appear to be facts from possibilities, and these in turn from norms or standards. Thus, a question about the yield of a particular crop may be answered with a hyphenated measure referring to the occurrence of such a yield (*don poti jhālī*), or to the regular (i.e., typical) occurrence of such a yield (*don poti hotāt/miltāt*), or to the predictable amount of the yield (*don poti milel*). These locutions are frequently used interchangeably without any systematic effort to distinguish them conceptually. Of course, this terminological ambiguity varies somewhat in regard to issues involving the past as opposed to the future, but this is more a grammatical than a conceptual qualification. Of course, under heavy prodding by the investigator, farmers are willing to specify which of these they actually mean in any given context (fact; possibility; regularity), and further can be coaxed to substitute single measures for hyphenated ranges, as they doubtless are frequently made to do. The point is that in their everyday discourse with each other they neither feel nor exert pressure for such elimination of ambiguity.

This property of peasant discourse involving measurement might be briefly characterized by its preponderance of subjunctives (may be, might be, could be, might have been, could have been, etc.). This role of the subjunctive mood in the language of measurement has implications for the relationship between measures and standards in such a system, which are explored in a later section. For the moment, it is simply worth remarking that the frequent use of hyphenated measures is not a direct function of uncertainty, variability, and fluctuation in the measurable environment but of these factors culturally mediated through a terminology that tends to conflate specific events, their ranges of possibility, the regularities which typify them, and the standards to which they ought to conform.

In a world dominated by measurement as approximation, farmers are frequently self-conscious and aware of this dimension of their everyday discourse. As a result, a kind of metalanguage of approximation has evolved, which is employed in much discourse regarding measurement.

Thus, farmers frequently use the word *andāj* (meaning rough or approximate) to qualify this or that proposition. Thus, it may be said that last year's yield of sorghum was roughly (*andāje*) 2–3 *poti* or that the almanac gives them a rough idea of when to expect rainfall (*panchāngātun pāvsāchā andāj milte*). Related terms in this metalanguage of approximation are *javal-javal* (near-about), *kamī-jāsta* (more or less), and, in the case of more sophisticated villages, *sarāsarī* (average). Used in combination with the grammar of the subjunctive, discussed previously, these terms punctuate the language of measurement and draw even the most precise assertions into the world of the approximate. Measurement as approximation implies a certain kind of social and cultural world which is discussed in the following section.

Measurement as Negotiation

Given the intimate link of local modes of measurement to practical contexts and their frequent expression in the language of the approximate, it further follows that the activity of measurement is, in a very important sense, a social activity. Given the paucity of abstract standards and the dearth of instruments distinct from the objects they are meant to measure, individuals are not perceived to have direct or independent access to the measures of their environment. Measurement, therefore, is always seen as a matter of opinion, and rarely as a matter of firm, or final, or indisputable knowledge. This is simply a different perspective on the terminology of the subjunctive discussed in the previous section. This terminology, by its very nature, is the language of uncertainty and of estimation. By extension, either explicitly or implicitly, it belongs to the idiom of give and take, of debate, of negotiation. This is always implicit in discussions of measurement. But it is frequently explicit.

The contrast between measurement as opinion and measurement as knowledge is not simply a surface characteristic of rural discourse, but I think characterizes an important set of implicit epistemological assumptions about the limits on the knowability of certain phenomena. Given the various characteristics of the ethos of rural measurement discussed earlier, it makes sense that measurement can never be certain, and the capacity to measure is rarely subject to the kind of technical and abstract methods which make it equally, and impersonally, available to each person. Whether by consensus, or by conflict, measurement is always a social activity, in which persons pool their respective estimates to arrive at some final, socially sanctioned estimate. In their culturally and experimentally ossified forms such estimates become standards, quantitative products of a particular social, cultural, and historical experience of a given environment.

The exchange of estimates almost always characterizes discussions about measure. But even when there is no explicit discussion of measures, negotiation and a potential plurality of estimates is always acknowledged. This does not mean that the tone of such opinions, for example when farmers are discussing the yields of hybrid grains on a particular piece of land, is always hesitant or tentative. Opinions can be held deeply and voiced dogmatically. But it is recognized that other opinions are always possible in most matters of measurement. So also, the opinion of some (believed to be wiser, shrewder, older, better informed, etc.) may affect the final consensus more than that of others, but it is precisely the social role of the various opinion-holders and the social framework of the particular context which determines the consensus measure, rather than reference to any abstract, context-free, value-neutral standard, or instrument of measure. This is as true of discussion about yields, prices, and crop mixtures, as it is of debate about landholdings, village population figures, or frequency of rainfall.

It is, of course, true that the more public, collective, and aggregate the phenomenon, the more its measurement consists of opinions, and the more private, individual, and singular the phenomenon, the more its measures are likely to be spoken of as matters of "fact" and not of opinion. But this is only tendency, and it is very rarely that the matters of measurement are regarded entirely as matters of fact. Thus, it is not at all rare for a question regarding the age of a particular individual to lead to a lively discussion, in which the respondent himself is accorded no special epistemic privilege and is viewed as expressing one legitimate opinion among many. Thus, when the investigator encounters a particular measure (say of the population of the village) invariably in his discussions, it is not so much because this measure is a product of some context-free tool of enumeration, but rather because there is such complete agreement on it that opinions on it have become standardized, and the fact has become, in Pierre Bourdieu's sense, "official."

If this analysis of the socially negotiated nature of measurement is reasonable, then it follows that the frequently noted "bargaining" or "haggling" characteristic of premodern bazaar behavior is not simply a function of imperfect markets and socially embedded economic transactions but is rooted in the idea that all measurement is opinion and all valuation is negotiable. Similarly, it has frequently been noted that in dispute settlement in peasant contexts, the effort is frequently to arrive at a socially acceptable compromise rather than an abstract "just" decision. What has not been so clearly seen is that measurement itself is a socially negotiated activity, no more subject to abstract measures than other matters of dispute or debate.

Conclusion

It would have been natural to conclude this chapter with some discussion of the relationship between measurement and social change in Vadi, but any detailed discussion of this topic would be out of place, since almost four decades have lapsed since I conducted the fieldwork on which this chapter is based, and I have not had a chance to go back to Vadi. In any case, the short duration of fieldwork is hardly the best lens into this kind of change, which involves small and subtle shifts over large spans of time. But a few comments may not be inappropriate. Vadi, like rural communities all over the world, is now subject to stronger and more rapid external forces than ever before. Banks and markets, clocks and calendars, surveys and salaries, census forms and ration cards, electric pumps and electricity bills, fertilizer factories, and radios: each of these, over the last decades, represents new symbols of precision in a world of approximation. Common to many of these agents of precision is the phenomenon of cash, the rapid process of monetization of a subsistence economy. On the whole, however, it seems as if growing precision in the standards and instruments of measurement had not in the early 1980s significantly affected the mentality of calculation and the ethos of measurement.

This ethos remains rooted in agricultural practices and conceptions which are of considerable antiquity. The language of measurement continues to blur the line between standards and instruments as well as between instruments and the object to be measured. The grammar of this language continues to be dominated by approximation, and the activity of measurement is still regarded as subject to social negotiation, rather than to abstract, independent, or context-free standards. Such shifts as have occurred are largely shifts in vocabulary: kilos have replaced seers and maunds, hectares sometimes replace acres and gunthas, Western names for months occasionally replace their indigenous counterparts. But the larger ethos of measurement, as it has been described in this chapter, changes slowly and imperceptibly. For those of us who practice a social science based on quite other ideas of measurement, some rethinking of method appears to be indicated.

CHAPTER 2

Small-Scale Techniques and Large-Scale Objectives

My objective in writing this essay is not to offer any new wisdom on the thorny problems of comparing and integrating the methods and results of work done on rural economic change at the macro and micro levels. My purposes are: (1) to raise a set of conceptual issues (many of them familiar to students of rural economic change in India); (2) to place them in an anthropological perspective; (3) to reflect on my own efforts to integrate qualitative and numerical work at the village level; (4) to suggest some hypotheses about the divergence between results at the two levels; (5) to propose a specific strategy for improved dialogue between analysts working at disparate levels; and (6) to provide an analysis of the reasons why such dialogue faces certain major obstacles. A word about my own qualifications: I have worked as an anthropologist at the village level in Maharashtra, and, though I am not entirely innumerate, I am largely a passive consumer of aggregate, numerical analyses of rural India. However, I am committed to criticism and improvement of approaches at *all* levels.

Some Terminological Clarifications

The terms "micro" and "macro" have a technical meaning in neoclassical economics, but there is apparently no simple or straightforward agreement as to what exactly that meaning is, even among economists. What is clear is that the loose sense in which the softer social sciences use these terms (to mean something like large- vs. small-scale) is confusing (and therefore unacceptable) to most economists, whose use of the terms does not necessarily have anything to do with scale. If, for purposes of clarity, we drop the terms "micro" and "macro," we are left with three pairs of terms that seem to cluster together in certain standard ways in discussions of the methodology of the study of rural economic change. They are: (1) small- versus large-scale; (2) qualitative versus quantitative; and (3) aggregative versus non-aggregative. Put crudely, village studies by anthropologists tend to be small-scale, qualitative, and non-aggregative; village studies by economists and agronomists (such as those conducted by the International Crops Research Institute for the Semi-Arid Tropics [ICRISAT] and the Agro-Economic Research Centres) tend to be small- or medium-scale, quantitative and aggregative; and large-scale studies (such as those of the National Sample Survey [NSS]) tend to be large-scale, quantitative and aggregative. Though there are exceptions to this general characterization, it seems fair to say that not much systematic thought has been given in studies of rural economic change in India (or elsewhere) to how we might break this conventional lumping of small-scale, non-aggregative and qualitative approaches on the one hand, and large-scale, aggregative and quantitative approaches on the other. In the final section of this essay I shall propose a relatively new strategy. But first we need to cover some more familiar ground.

Mutual Criticisms

There is no need to go over in detail the criticisms made by practitioners at large and small scales of each others' methods and interpretations. Criticism of the deficiencies of large-scale survey research has a long history (see, for example, Leach 1967; Gibson and Hawkins 1968; Srinivas 1979; Zeller and Carmines 1980) and in recent times there have been several discussions of the problems of exporting Western survey techniques to the Third World (Mitchell 1965; Hursh-Cesar and Roy 1976). A recent essay by Stone and Campbell (1984) summarizes many of these problems and proposes an interesting strategy for using these approaches in a complementary manner. Criticisms of village-level anthropological work by those working at larger scales and with quantitative techniques are less frequently published, but are no less harsh. On the one side, there are accusations of losing cultural salience, processual links, and relational information. On the other side, there is the problem of non-quantifiability, indefinite representativeness, and limited comparability. Less noted is the fact that village-level anthropological work frequently does not overlap in *content* with the concerns of the large-scale surveys. In general, until recently, anthropological work at the village level in India did not focus on problems of agricultural life, economic opportunities, and standards of living.

But there have recently been a variety of signs of efforts to link village studies with studies undertaken at larger scales. These include the VLS (Village-Level Studies) undertaken by ICRISAT since 1976; the work of the Agro-Economic Research Centres in India; the work in Bengal of Ashok Rudra and Pranab Bardhan, and of CRESSIDA;[1] the work of some individual scholars (Mencher 1978; Étienne 1982; J. Harriss 1982; Hill 1982), and the work of scholars associated with B. H. Farmer in Sri Lanka and South India (Farmer 1977; Bayliss-Smith and Wanmali 1984). The purposes of these individuals and institutions vary greatly and it is only in some of these cases that the use of village-level data to make larger-scale arguments is a central objective. In the discussion that follows, I have been influenced by data and techniques contained in these studies, but I shall not cite them extensively.

In order for there to be any worthwhile cooperation between analysts working at the village level and those working at larger scales, village-level studies, especially those conducted by anthropologists, must focus, at least in part, on rural economic life. One very detailed blueprint for what exactly this means is contained in the *Manual of Instructions for Economic Investigators in ICRISAT's Village Level Studies* (Binswanger and Jodha 1978), though aspects of the underlying approach of this manual could be subject to the criticisms recently made by John Harriss

---

1. CRESSIDA: The Centre for Regional, Ecological, and Science Studies in Development Alternatives, Calcutta, India. Four volumes, including one double one, have been published. The first two are entitled *CRESSIDA Transactions* (Vol. I, No. 1, Summer 1981, 232 pp.; No. 2, Winter 1981, 250 pp.); the others are entitled *Ecoscience, CRESSIDA Transactions* (Vol. II, 1982, special issue, Nos. 1 and 2, 382 pp.; Vol. III, Summer 1983, No. 1, 234 pp.). Address: CRESSIDA, Chaturanga, 32 Govinda Auddy Road, Calcutta 700027. The four volumes will be referred to hereafter conventionally by the title *CRESSIDA* followed by the number of the volume, the year, and the page numbers.

(1983) of the village studies of the Agro-Economic Research Centre in Visva Bharti, West Bengal. For those particularly interested in contractual aspects of rural agricultural life, an excellent model is to be found in Rudra and Bardhan (1983). What needs to be emphasized is that these are models for capturing data concerning certain relationships. But a general model of Indian villages as economies and of agriculture regarded as a social form is only gradually beginning to emerge (Bliss and Stern 1982; J. Harriss 1982, 1983; Desai, Rudolph, and Rudra 1984), though there have been important earlier steps in this direction (Epstein 1962, 1973; Beteille 1974; Breman 1974; Mencher 1978). Thus, the analysis of rural economy by anthropologists is not just a matter of looking at the right things, but also of evolving an appropriate theory of the village as an agrarian economy. It is worth noting, in this context, a series of recent arguments to the effect that although Indian villages are not autonomous as in the nineteenth-century administrative myth, they are nevertheless coherent, significant, and fairly well-bounded locations for social and economic processes (Schlesinger 1981; J. Harriss 1983; Rudra 1984). But this sort of coherence does not necessarily support the sort of "holism" traditionally guiding the work of anthropologists (see the last section of this essay). Thus, the fear that anthropologists were confined to an arbitrary and meaningless locus of human activity—the village—seems to have been premature.

There is an inverse problem at the level of the large-scale survey. On the whole (and here the National Survey Sample is the outstanding example), the statistical sophistication of these studies is not matched by the richness or sophistication of the macro-sociological theory underlying the statistical work. Nor is this simply the charge of what to do about "non-sampling" error, something of which statisticians involved with large-scale survey work, especially in India, are very aware, and others frequently remind them. The problem is more basic.

Deficiencies in Large-Scale Studies

To my knowledge, there has been no explicit discussion of the *macro-sociological* foundations that underlie the economics, which in turn underpin the statistical techniques on which these surveys are based. That is, what is the model of social structure, of social relations, and of social processes that justifies what is being measured and how it is being measured, in these surveys? The partial exception to this involves the very lively debates surrounding poverty and income distribution (Srinivasan, Srinivasan, and Bardhan 1974; Dandekar 1981; Sen 1981; Sukhatme 1981) but even these debates have been more precisely terminological and methodological, rather than theoretical. Let me suggest two major inadequacies in the sociological basis of most large-scale survey work in India. In common with most large-scale surveys whose minimal unit is the "household" or the family, Indian surveys assume that these units are *formally independent* loci of action and of choice, even if they differ in various endowments (such as income, family size, etc.). But a large amount of sociological and anthropological work in India (and not all of it "Marxist") shows that unequal and reciprocal relations *between* households are central to the "choices" made by actors and to their reasons for these choices. These highly localized structural relationships between households are not merely masked by the techniques of most large-scale surveys but are virtually incompatible with their basic sociological assumptions. Indeed, to the degree that the entire country is regarded as an *aggregation* of households, the large-scale surveys (however statistically sophisticated) will inevitably end up with data that is *distributional* rather than *relational*.

Since the contrast between distributional and relational data (and models) is the key to the proposal with which I shall conclude this essay, let me briefly discuss its implications. All aggregate data-gathering techniques associated with neoclassical economic assumptions regard the critical data regarding standard of living as contained in *measurable distributions* of goods, usually at the household level. There are a few exceptions to this, particularly in its Marxist variant. Though Marxian economists have concentrated on *relations* between groups (usually classes), rather than simply on distributions of goods and services, they have not been able to translate this sociological critique into a methodological alternative to current methods and models for the aggregation of data concerning standard of living. In general, they use data generated by standard statistical methods in order to conduct debates with neoclassical economists about the interpretation of these data. Thus, the relational bias of Marxism, with which I am fully in sympathy, does not provide a real alternative to the problem of effective aggregation without the sacrifice of the relational perspective.

The recent survey research by Bardhan and Rudra at the intermediate levels of rural society in Bengal constitutes a promising start for breaking through the impressions that relational approaches and aggregate analyses are mutually exclusive. Yet though their approach, especially in regard to tenancy and labor, is admirably relational it too remains confined to *outcomes* of social processes, rather than to the structure of those processes themselves. When I discuss my own approach to "entitlement events," in a later section of this essay, this observation will be clarified.

The challenge is not just to capture social relations at the large scale through surveys conducted at smaller levels (a problem which is hardly simple in itself). Nor is it only a matter of having a more articulate (and thus debatable) general social theory at the locus of the design of the large-scale surveys, though this too would be helpful. The problem, at least in regard to rural economic change in India, is how to build a model of *standard of living*, which is not a mechanical aggregation of easily quantifiable bundles of goods and services (quantities of food, medicine, education, shelter, sanitation, etc.).

This is not the place for a full-scale review of the extensive literature on the "standard of living," its measurement and operationalization. But a few points are worth making. Few will deny that to the degree that measures of standards of living are studied in the aggregate, they tend to lose the critical qualitative dimension which must belong to any robust conception of the standard of living. Components of this qualitative dimension include: the perception of security in livelihood, the sense of freedom from harassment and abuse at home and at work, the feeling of dignity in day-to-day transactions, the belief in the reliability of officialdom, the expectation (or lack of it) that life will improve for one's offspring, and so forth. The fact that these are matters that are not easy to operationalize for the purposes of large-scale survey work does not make them sentimental issues, irrelevant to the understanding of rural economy. It does mean, however, that our macro-sociological theory must take into account "well-being" as well as "welfare" (here I borrow the contrast from Das and Nicholas 1985); "subjective" as well as "objective" criteria of "well-being"; and emotional and ideological states as much as bundles of commodities. To use another set of terms which I have paired in another context, it is essential not simply to look at "entitlement" (Sen 1981) but also at "enfranchisement" (Appadurai 1984a).

The second inadequacy in current macro-sociological theory regarding rural economic change involves a problem created at the intersection of *scale and aggregation*. There is no single term or concept which captures this particular problem, but important aspects of it have been dealt with by Jon Elster (1979), Fred Hirsch (1976), and Thomas Schelling (1978). In its simplest form, the problem is that the aggregate outcome of a series of identical (from the micro point of view) actions may be a macro pattern which frustrates "micro motives." There are many examples of such "ironies of aggregation"[2] and their analysis brings together problems of scale, interaction and "centricity" (Hannerz 1979) in social life.

In order to clarify my view of such ironies of aggregation, to which I shall return in a later section of this essay, let me draw on an example, based on my field experience in Maharashtra. In many parts of Maharashtra, as well as in other areas of scarce or unreliable water supply, open-surface (dug) wells are a critical component of agricultural technology. In Maharashtra, in the last few decades, many small farmers have taken to devoting small portions of their holdings to commercial crops. In many cases, they do so by investing in electric (or diesel) pumps in order to draw water more efficiently onto their plots. The objective, for most farmers, in investing in commercial agriculture even with tiny plots, uncertain labor and fluctuating prices, is two-fold: (a) to maximize cash income in an increasingly monetized environment; and (b) to gradually accumulate enough cash to increase their irrigated landholdings. The objective of many small farmers (seen at the micro level) is to achieve economic independence from other farmers as well as nonfarmers and to be in a position where they can operate independently of small-scale cooperative organizations. Yet given the smallness of their individual plots—the fact that they often have to invest in electrical pumps *jointly*, and the fact that they all experience the most intense needs for cash, water, and labor at approximately the same periods in the agricultural calendar, they are inevitably drawn into highly interdependent webs of debt, bullock-sharing, and water-sharing. Especially for smaller farmers, this interdependence at the village level, which often creates bottlenecks which impede production, tends to diminish their commercial incomes and in the long run to reduce their chances of economic autonomy. Thus, the micro motive—to achieve long-term independence by investing in commercial agriculture—often leads, at the macro level, to bottlenecks and failures which assure continuing reliance of small farmers on each other and on bigger farmers.

This tension between micro motives and macro outcomes has important implications for the measurement of rural economic change. It means that we need to be skeptical about interpreting increases in certain aggregate measures, such as number of wells, number of electric pumps, acreage of irrigated land, or yields of commercial crops, as

---

2.   I owe this evocative phrase to Ulf Hannerz.

automatically an index of increase in well-being at the micro level. Nor is this only because such increases can disguise increases in the concentration of agricultural capital in the hands of a small rural elite. What it can also disguise, at least in certain parts of rural India, is an increasingly involuted agrarian landscape in which irrigated, commercial agriculture implies a large number of *small* commercial farmers eking out a precarious subsistence in a heavily monetized agrarian economy. To analyze this particular irony of aggregation properly it is important to look, at the village level, at the full *relational* implications of petty commercialization.[3]

Economists have long been aware that any macro perspective implies, methodologically, some understanding of the aggregation process. Neoclassical theory, both in its understanding of equilibrium and in its conceptualization of externalities, recognizes the complexity of the relationship between micro behaviors and the context within which they occur. But most economists would concede that it is illegitimate to postulate algebraic homologies between micro variables and their macro counterparts and that it is difficult to work out the aggregate implications of specific micro relationships. One solution, essentially based on a number-crunching approach, would be through computer simulation of the aggregation process based on the numerical specification of the values involved in micro relationships. In addition to the massive magnitude of computations involved, I believe this method rests on an approach to measurement which seeks to quantify essentially qualitative social facts. But I would like to suggest that another way to illuminate the aggregation process would rely on relatively standard analytic/sampling techniques but build them on an alternative approach to observation and measurement. This alternative approach, discussed more fully in a subsequent section of this essay, would be built on the assumption that social life is constituted by a series of small-scale interactions in which large-scale factors are embedded, rather than by large-scale factors as such.

This aspect of social life is precisely what is unlikely to be captured in the current methodologies of large-scale survey research, not simply because of problems of method but because no persuasive theory of this feature of large-scale social phenomena currently exists. It is worth paying particular attention to this dimension of the relationship between small- and large-scale phenomena, for here is a problem to which

---

3.   For a fuller treatment of the microsociology of irrigation in rural Maharashtra, see Appadurai 1984c [chapter 3 in this volume].

conventional survey approaches *as well as* conventional anthropological approaches have no obvious solution. It is thus a prime justification for cooperation. The question, of course, is how is it to be operationalized in the study of rural economic change? But before this question can be addressed, it is necessary to turn the critical spotlight onto how anthropologists have generally fared in their study of rural economic life.

Limitations of Village Studies

By and large, village studies in India have been undertaken by anthropologists and sociologists, although the study of villages by economists and agronomists has a fairly long history (see, for example, Slater 1918 and Mann 1967). The bulk of these studies, conducted largely after World War II, paid cursory attention if any to rural economic life, apart from certain aspects of it, such as the so-called *"jajmani"* system. The problem in regard to the *systematic* study of change is doubly vexed. Longitudinal research is still in its infancy in social anthropology at large (see, for example, Foster et al. 1979) and in India, with a few notable exceptions, such as Scarlett Epstein (1962, 1973) and, more recently, Murray Leaf (1984), there have been few "re-studies" of particular villages. So far, therefore, anthropologists working at the village level have not had much to say about rural economic change.

But even at the impressionistic level, there is an emerging consensus among some anthropologists that things have improved over the last few decades. It is worth asking why this impression should exist, especially in the face of a fair amount of data to the opposite effect.

Let me suggest the following reasons for this tendency on the part of some anthropologists to assess rural economic change in India in a positive manner. The *first* is the tendency (following a variety of official and semi-official cues) for anthropologists to end up in villages that are in largely prosperous regions, or in highly developed pockets in poorer regions. The *second* is the tendency to miss serious economic downturns in the seasonal cycles of the places they study (Chambers 1983). The *third* is the tendency to become restricted to the world of the powerful and the prosperous unless, as in the case of Kathleen Gough (1981), a major effort is made in the reverse direction. The *fourth* reason is that since they are trained to use their eyes as well as their ears (and perhaps because of an unconscious interest in what used to be called "material culture"), anthropologists tend to be excessively impressed by the presence of new commodities and increased amounts of them: watches, bicycles, and radios are particularly damaging in this regard, for anthropologists are usually ill-equipped to measure the net costs of aggregate increases in such commodities, costs reflected in the gradual immiseration of some families, the hidden toll of migration and monetization on family life, etc. This fourth factor is exacerbated by a version of factor three, which is that people who are temporarily or permanently suffering an economic downturn sometimes vanish from just those casual, public, interactional arenas in which anthropologists conduct their "participant-observation." They may retreat to their homes or they may leave the village suddenly and surreptitiously. Such small social demographic shifts in a single village are often the surface symptoms of rural stress. A *fifth* problem is more subtle: the random observations and free-floating dyadic exchanges in which anthropologists gather most of their "data" are likely to encourage optimistic assessments of their situation by many respondents/informants. This can be a function of pride in the village (which can be a surprisingly important ideological factor) or of embarrassment about discussing bad fortune in the presence of friends and neighbors who are often present at such exchanges. Finally, the short time-frame in which much anthropological fieldwork is conducted means that it is difficult for the analysts as well as the actors to assess "trends" correctly. The fifth factor should not be overemphasized, for Indian villagers can also, for a variety of reasons (ranging from fear of the evil eye, the tax-collector, or the motives of the anthropologist) exaggerate their poverty or ill-fortune. But anthropologists (for some reason) tend to reserve their skepticism for exaggerations of the latter rather than the former sort!

These are some general (and easily recognized) reasons that anthropologists might tend to assess rural economic change in a positive manner, however impressionistic their methods. But even if they were to resolve to guard against these dangers, and revise their priorities to pay more focused attention to rural economic life, there are serious methodological problems with the systematic study of agricultural economy at the village level. I shall draw upon my own experience in Maharashtra in 1981–82 to highlight a few of these.

A Case Study of Village-Level Economic Research

In 1981–82 I spent ten months doing intensive research on agricultural decision-making in a village (with the pseudonym Vadi) in Purandhar taluq, Pune district, Maharashtra state. Approximately three of these months were spent in doing research that must be described as preliminary. Another three months were spent in designing and supervising the administration of a fairly elaborate survey of all 193 households in the village. The remaining four months were spent in intensive interviewing and observation, both formal and informal, of the standard anthropological variety. I was assisted in these activities by no more than two research assistants at any time, so this was a small-scale research enterprise in every sense of the term. This study is still one of a relatively small number of efforts in India (1) to attempt the anthropological study of a localized agrarian social order, and (2) to attempt a reasonably intensive combination of survey research with ethnographic research. Thus I believe there is some justification in using some of my experiences as springboards for general discussion. I will not detail some of the standard problems I encountered in designing and implementing my research plans, which have been discussed by many others. I will stress that, like most researchers, I had to learn to be flexible and adjust my goals and interests continuously, as some doors opened and others closed. What I shall discuss below are four sets of problems which are less commonly discussed. They are as follows: (1) problems of agricultural terminology; (2) problems involving measurement; (3) problems involving the boundedness of the village as an agrarian social order; and (4) problems involving the timing and duration of qualitatively-oriented survey work. These are discussed serially in what follows.

(1) *Agricultural terminology.* All intensive local-level work, whether its focus is qualitative or quantitative, involves the solution of linguistic problems, even when native speakers are involved in the research. The linguistic problems faced by survey researchers in Third World countries are only beginning to be discussed, and it has been noted in the Nepali context that there are inevitable gaps between the literate varieties of languages used in questionnaires and the local spoken varieties (Shrestha 1979) and that there are also more subtle problems of how specific words or turns of phrase may be reinterpreted by informants, leading to unintended misinformation (Stone and Campbell 1984). Nor is this simply a "Third-World" problem (Schuman and Presser 1981; Fienberg, Loftus, and Tanur 1984).

In the study of local agrarian systems, there are problems that represent special forms of the linguistic problems involved in all rural research. In a different context, it has been found convenient to label these as problems of "agricultural terminology."[4] I shall mention here only two terminological problems that seem especially relevant to the linkage of village-level studies with studies conducted at a larger scale.

Perhaps the least discussed aspect of agricultural terminology is the variable geographical spread of key agricultural terms. While certain Marathi terms used by farmers appear to be extremely wide in their geographical spread, others appear to be localized to one district or parts of a few districts. Thus, the term *ardholi* (or some recognizable cognate of this term) seems to refer to a crop-sharing arrangement in which the partners have 50/50 shares throughout the Marathi-speaking region. But the term *varangula* is used where I worked for certain forms of agricultural partnership, involving the pooling of bullocks and plowing equipment, whereas in Satara district the term *payra* is used for a substantially similar arrangement (Schlesinger 1981). Furthermore, these terms are apparently not even recognized outside their respective area of use. Such examples of varying terminological micro-regions can probably be multiplied, but in the absence of a systematic survey of terminological variation we can only guess at its nature and extent. This terminological variation, even *within* linguistic regions, has a series of implications relevant to this discussion. First, it means that even questionnaires designed with the help of persons who have prior rural experience in the broad linguistic region are likely to use inappropriate agricultural terms. Second, it means that the problem of quantifying (or even comparing) the incidences of certain kinds of agrarian arrangements is compounded by such terminological variation. The inverse form of this problem is the existence of a common term to describe what are in fact divergent practices. Third, it means that intensive agricultural research in any given village or locality must involve a careful preliminary period of observation and interviewing simply to establish a basic and accurate lexicon of key local agricultural terms. I shall return to this last issue when I discuss the problem of the timing and duration of survey work on rural economies.

(2) *Measurement*. I have discussed elsewhere, at some length, the practical and epistemological problems raised in the analysis of rural agricultural discourse involving measurement (Appadurai 1984b [see chapter 1, this volume]). I shall mention here only a few points which are

---

4.   The Social Science Research Council (USA) has hosted a series of conferences on "Agricultural Terminology," where this topic has been explored in greater detail.

particularly relevant to this discussion. I am not concerned here with the problem of deliberate misrepresentation of magnitudes (of land, income, property, debt, etc.) by respondents, nor about errors in measurement (in the standard sense) by investigators. I am concerned with intercultural gaps in usage and interpretation. In my fieldwork, I found that there was an almost invariable tendency to represent magnitudes qualitatively and comparatively ("enough," "more than last year," "as much as I had hoped for," etc.) rather than quantitatively. Further, when quantities were described, there was a strong tendency to use what I have called "hyphenated measures" (seven–eight, ten–twelve, twenty–thirty, etc.) especially in regard to plot sizes and crop yields, but also in regard to other matters. When precise numerical replies are given, they frequently reflect "official" or "standardized" numbers rather than individual assessments: this is especially true of demographic inquiries. Finally, discussions of measure, which are frequently public and collective (especially in formal interview contexts) involve social consensus about magnitudes and not reference to context-free tools of measurement. In all these regards, the relatively technical, quantitative, and context-free assumptions of most interviewers regarding measurements are directly opposed to the more relational, qualitative, approximate, and context-tied discourse of rural respondents. In most rural survey work this contradiction is "cleaned-up" in the interest of yielding usable (but often simply inaccurate) numerical data. The problem of designing surveys which can accommodate fuzzy and approximate quantitative responses (especially in regard to production and consumption data) has hardly been addressed anywhere. Of course, there are other contexts, typically involving demographic and marketing issues, where careful questioning (and cross-checks) can *legitimately* and usefully eliminate much ambiguity. Thus, the central challenge in this area is how to commensurate the structure of farmers' discourse involving measure with the very different requirements (at least at present) of large-scale surveys.

(3) *The boundedness of the rural economy.* The problem of the sense in which the local agrarian economy is a bounded entity involves difficult decisions about the local "unit of analysis" which in turn affects problems of aggregation and of large-scale analysis. I have already mentioned some recent reactions to the overemphasis on the non-boundedness of the village, and a revival of interest in the village as a coherent and significant locus of agrarian organization. In general I am sympathetic with the recent arguments that the village should not be too easily dissolved

into a larger interactional framework (Schlesinger 1981; J. Harriss 1983; Rudra 1984).

Based on my own fieldwork, the major preliminary challenge is how to develop some typology (however rough) of villages which classifies them according to the degree that they are relatively autonomous economic entities. In making this assessment, it would be essential to distinguish the village as a *polity* from the village as an *economy*. In the latter regard, the critical dimensions of linkage with the larger economy would have to do with (a) extent of outmigration of males or females, which affects local labor patterns as well as local monetization levels, and (b) extent of commercialization of agriculture, which also ties local to regional economies. Of course, such a typology can be based on criteria and measures of varying degrees of sophistication, but some such typology would be essential in the sampling that underlies any large-scale survey work on the rural economy, in addition to regional variations of the sort that can already be disaggregated from the data of the large-scale surveys. My own very impressionistic hypothesis is that, over the last few decades, dramatic increases in the ranges of income are likely to have occurred in villages more closely tied to the regional and national economy, whereas the picture of changes would be flatter in villages which are less affected by the labor and commodity needs of regional systems. Put another way, "satellite" villages are more likely to show misleading signs of prosperity but be subject to deeper disparities in income than more (economically speaking) remote villages. From the point of view of integrating village-level analysis with large-scale surveys, the first methodological step would be to develop a model of village independence through intensive village-level research which could be used in subsequent sampling for the purpose of providing more sensitive information on rural economic change.

It is especially difficult for anthropologists to follow those processes and individuals that lead outside the village. My own experience in the village I studied was that it was very difficult to follow through *anthropologically* the two key links between the village I studied and the larger regional economy. The first involved the study of the economic and social structure of the domestic economies (especially in Mumbai) of those families that maintained dual budgetary loci. This would have entailed an extended stay in Mumbai which was practically unfeasible. But, in the future, it will be essential that at least some "village" studies focus specifically on the "dual-loci" households that increasingly character-ize "satellite" villages all over India. Except for migration studies (which have a very different thrust) there exists now virtually no method for the micro-sociology of such spatially bifurcated social units. Similarly, a full study of the impact of the commercialization of agriculture would have required understanding and following in detail the ties of farmers in Vadi to specific wholesalers in the vegetable and fruit markets of Mumbai and Pune, ties which affect credit, volume of production, acreage under commercial cropping, and reliability of profit. This too is something, due to limitations of time and resources, I was unable to do. But it should be noted that the *anthropological* study of such *trans-local* social and economic processes is also in its conceptual infancy.

(4) *Timing and duration of survey work.* At least among anthropologists, there is rarely much public discussion of research design and method. But a customary set of practices does exist, and this set requires rethinking, if anthropologists are to make any serious contribution to the study of rural economic change. Most anthropologists engaged in village-level work tend to conduct survey work (usually involving a simple census of households along with some preliminary genealogical work) at the *outset* of their research period, which is rarely more than a year. The result is that such surveys, even when they do concern matters of rural economics, are conducted during the period when the anthropologist is an *outsider*, in every sense. This is the phase when he might be weakest in the local language, most uneasy about his links to the community, shaky in his relations with his own research assistants, and when his own assistants are in the delicate process of building their own relations with the community. In regard to rural economies, specifically, this means that the survey is designed and implemented when the investigator's knowledge of the *specific* local structure, rhythm, and terminology of the economy is most shaky.

My own approach in Vadi was to spend the first two months in informal interviewing and observation, with an eye to identifying the critical *local* dimensions of the agricultural system and in discovering the appropriate *local* way to phrase questions concerning them. I then spent one month designing and translating into Marathi a lengthy questionnaire (which had both numerical as well as qualitative dimensions). Each questionnaire took about two hours to administer and though I had two full-time assistants (who did about 3–4 households each per working day), it took almost two months for all 193 households to be covered. It then took another month to deal with ambiguities, errors, and gaps. Thus, the administration of the survey took almost three out of the total of ten months of my research. However, in the last five months my focused ethnographic interviewing, with a purposive sampling of households, was greatly facilitated by what I had learned (and failed to learn) in the course of administering the survey, though the analysis had to wait until after the completion of the field research. This procedure is one that I would recommend as superior to the traditional anthropological practice of having survey work precede intensive ethnographic work. The essential features of this approach are: (1) to do the survey work in the *middle* months of the allotted research time, to assure that the questionnaire is as culturally sensitive as possible and that the lessons learned during its administration can be applied in the final months of the research period, which are for anthropologists traditionally the most profitable. I should, of course, point out that this procedure is not intended to solve all the problems of combining quantitative and qualitative work on village economies, but is only intended to address the problems of timing and duration, and these too in only one regard. The purpose of these reflections on my own problems (and solutions) in the course of doing village-level anthropological research on agriculture was to suggest some areas for future discussion on how anthropological contributions to such studies might be improved. But the question of the link between small- and large-scale studies can now be addressed more directly.

Linkage Between Levels: A Methodological Proposal

The reader should by now be aware that I feel a great deal remains to be done at *both* levels in order for work at the village level to be fruitfully integrated with work at larger scales. What I wish to do in this concluding section is to make a specific proposal for a research strategy which might be one among several formats for cooperation. Since this is an idea which I have only recently begun to consider, I warn the reader not to expect it to be completely clear or fully worked out. It is presented as an idea-in-progress. But first a word about the context. Although contrasting and integrating research conducted at different levels and scales is a central problem of the social sciences, surprisingly little methodological attention has been paid to it, and what little has been written is scattered.[5] Speaking schematically, there seem to be three interesting

5.   Two landmark collections of essays which address the problem are: (1) *Scale and Social Organization*, edited by Fredrik Barth (1978), which

approaches to the problem of closing the gap between micro and macro approaches.

The *first*, which I have touched on already, sees the transition from micro to macro phenomena as involving not just problems of aggregation, but also of unintended consequences, and of analyzing the emergent properties of collective social forms which cannot be predicted from their micro-constituents. In addition to scholars like Elster, Hirsch, and Schelling, whom I have mentioned already in relation to the issue of the "ironies of aggregation," this approach is favored by methodologists such as Rom Harré (1981) and Anthony Giddens (1981). The problem with this approach is that it has not so far yielded any clear operational lessons, though its theoretical position is hard to challenge. In my earlier example of the ironies of aggregation involved in the commercialization of agriculture in Maharashtra, I did suggest one implication of this problem: namely that micro-facts have to be looked at *relationally*, rather than only distributionally, even at the micro level, in order to avoid false inferences at the macro level.

The *second* approach, which is narrow but very promising, comes out of Aaron Cicourel's important *Method and Measurement in Sociology* (1964) which set the grounds for a thoroughgoing micro-sociological critique of macro-sociology, in which Cicourel has himself played an important role. Cicourel's work criticized, firstly, existing methods of measurement in sociology, which relied on mathematical measurement requirements such as properties of scales that are hardly ever fulfilled with variables of the type used in traditional sociology. Second, Cicourel criticized methods which assumed that data, for example, collected in interviews, could be taken at face value (except for measurement error and bias, which, however, could be either statistically remedied or estimated). His own "micro-sociological perspective" sees such data as "unspecified collaborative products created during the interview in accordance with

---

consists largely of essays by anthropologists and thus is concerned largely with problems of scale as they affect the analysis of "simpler" and more "complex" societies, and (2) *Advances in Social Theory and Methodology: Towards an Integration of Micro- and Macro-Sociologies*, edited by Karin Knorr-Cetina and Aaron V. Cicourel (1981), which is written from a sociological and philosophical perspective. These two collections give a fairly good sampling of the range of approaches that the micro-macro problem has generated, in anthropology and sociology.

the practical procedures and background assumptions of participating actors" (Knorr-Cetina 1981: 13).

In his own recent work, Cicourel has suggested that an important way to identify those processes and inferences that transform micro-events into macro-structures is by looking at how certain routine problem-solving activities, in complex micro-settings, lead to the creation of macro-structures (Cicourel 1981: 67).[6]

The *third* approach, which underlies my own proposal, is very closely linked to Cicourel's micro-critique of macro-sociology, but takes an even more radical stance. It has been laid out by one of the more radical of the new "micro-sociologists," Randall Collins, in a series of papers (Collins 1981a, 1981b, 1983). Since my own suggestion is influenced in part by Collins, it is worth stating his proposal in some detail, and noting those features of it that I find especially congenial.

Collins is one of a group of "radical" micro-sociologists who are committed to some version of the idea that aggregate, collective, macro-phenomena are in large part artifacts of analysis and that "empirical" reality is invariably composed of large numbers of events that are small-scale, in terms of duration, spatial extension, and number of participants. With the exception of time, space, and number, which are the only genuine macro-variables admitted by Collins, the rest (examples would be "class," "state," "distribution of wealth," "mobility rate," etc.) are in fact simply concepts (used both by social scientists and actors) to gloss what are in

---

6.   The following lengthy quotation gives the flavor of Cicourel's strategy:
      Bureaucratic organizations typically produce reports of routine and special board-meetings, or meetings in which a group decides whether to give someone a loan, a grant or a fellowship. In medicine and law, patients and clients are interviewed and a medical history or legal statement or brief is prepared that summarizes an interview and the assessment of tests and documents. In all of these cases, and many more that can be easily identified as routine practices within bureaucratic organizations, there are fairly explicit procedures that have been adopted or that have emerged. This "rationalization" process has increased over the past 100 years and shows no signs of diminishing. Everyday settings, therefore, abound with highly organized ways of dealing with and producing macro-evaluations, reports and summarizations of relentless micro-events ... In each case the activities are routine aspects of some organization and are independent of the way social scientists design and carry out their research. (Cicourel 1981: 66)

fact complex chains of micro-events. In this view, a genuinely empirical sociology would not be a matter of using quantitative data, but of careful analysis of micro-events. For reasons that fall outside the scope of this discussion, the micro-events that most interest Collins are "conversations" in ordinary life situations, and his main methodological proposal for how to proceed with this radical micro-sociology involves the analysis of what he calls (following Goffman) "interaction rituals," in which individuals transact and exchange certain forms of emotional energy, conversational or cultural "capital," and their social reputation. Complex chains of such encounters "distribute and redistribute various micro-resources among the aggregate of individuals in a society" (Collins 1983: 192).

The systematic analysis of such micro-events is what Collins calls "micro-translation" (i.e., the translation of apparently macro-structures into their micro-constituents). He recognizes that, given the very large number of such micro-events that combine to form larger-scale phenomena, the central methodological issue is how to "sample" such micro-events, and in his most recent discussion of this approach he advocates "systematic sampling of certain microsituations" (Collins 1983: 195). However, he notes that there are serious challenges in sampling "situations," especially if our purposes are descriptive, since we know very little about the distribution of various kinds of micro-events there is no "census" of them from which a random sample can be drawn, etc. But more purposive sampling can illuminate the relationships among certain variables, even if the representativeness problem remains.

There are several problems with Collins's proposal for micro-sampling of interaction rituals (micro-events) as a way to create a genuinely empirical bridge between micro- and macro-sociology. These include: (a) a theoretical blindness to the sorts of "unintended consequences" that have been repeatedly shown to emerge in the course of aggregation and which sampling alone cannot capture; (b) an extremely positivist conception of social reality; (c) a lack of cross-cultural sensitivity in his specific proposals about authority, property, etc.; and (d) a poorly developed statistical approach to carry out his methodological program.

These shortcomings severely limit the viability of Collins's proposals for the purposes for which he intended them, namely as the basis for a radical reconstruction of sociology from the bottom up. But it is possible that his proposal *may* be applicable (with suitable refinements) to the problem with which we are most concerned at present: namely, how can micro and macro perspectives be better integrated in the study of rural economic change in India and of the changes in standards of living?

For our purposes, the critical feature of Collins's scheme is the emphasis on *sampling*, the shift from *distributions* to *interactions*, and the move from *interviews* to *observation and recording* of small pieces of naturally occurring behavior. The critical questions then become: (1) What micro-events or transactions are likely to be sensitive indices of rural standards of living? (2) What are the practical problems of observing and recording their structure without seriously interfering with them? and (3) What statistical methods can be employed both in the selection of such micro-events and in their subsequent aggregation? I am aware that each of these questions covers a host of more specific problems and puzzles, but at this stage they can only be discussed in very preliminary terms.

Question (1), about what micro-events or transactions are likely to be good indices of rural standards of living, can be rephrased as follows: is there a class of events that is a sensitive micro-indicator of (in Amartya Sen's terms) "entitlement-maps" (Sen 1981)? The areas of transaction and interaction that come to mind are: (a) *actual* labor contracts (i.e., the real transaction in which a specific contract is set); (b) in situations where rationing of essential commodities is in force, *observed* transactions in these commodities; (c) *efforts* to obtain credit from banks and cooperatives; and (d) specific acts of rural out-migration. The challenge is how to evolve a method for *observing* transactions of these types, since some of them happen outside official record-keeping contexts. This would require some hard thinking, and possibly the elimination of some possibilities.

What is the point of looking at such entitlement events close up rather than taking the usual approach of trying to capture the outcomes of such events through interviews involving formal survey instruments or through census-style inquiries? There would be at least three payoffs in examining the events themselves: (1) it might permit some insight into the *nature* of such events (i.e., a qualitative or *relational* insight) rather than only an insight into the *distributional* results of such events; (2) it might give a better understanding of *failures* in the entitlement arena, i.e., why certain persons or groups, in real situations, *fail* to get some good, service, or benefit, since the reasons may in part be based on very specific features (linguistic or otherwise) of the micro-situation itself; (3) in looking at actual negotiations or interactions involving livelihood, we may illuminate *aspirations* and *expectations* as well as *post facto* outcomes. In all these regards, this type of micro-scrutiny might add several important dimensions to the current forms of interview or census-generated material.

Further, even after a type (or several types) of entitlement event is identified as being relevant, observationally feasible, and in some way statistically manageable, the concrete question remains: what exactly will be recorded and how can personnel be trained to record relevant linguistic and micro-sociological details of these transactions? There, the trade-off is between the qualitative and unpredictable structure of these events, and the standardization of technique required for reasonable success. Here, too, I have no simple solutions but dialogue between specialists with different disciplinary strengths may be fruitful.

In addition to the construction of flexible but well-designed micro-protocols for the observation and recording of these small units of entitlement-related interactions, there remains the problem of the selection of a sample and of subsequent processing (for aggregate purposes) of the results. Though the statistical aspect may pose serious problems, the organizational aspect may be solved by having a few, limited, "pilot" projects of this sort attached to the ongoing, well-established activities of the National Sample Survey.

Nevertheless, in my judgment, the critical potential contribution of the analysis of entitlement events to improving the relationship between micro and macro analysis is not through (a) some miraculous resolution of the challenge of achieving a representative sample or (b) through some new angle on the thorny problem of unintended consequences. What it is likely to do is to contribute to the refinement of the macro theory which underlies analyses at the large-scale level. That is, by looking at entitlement events in addition to entitlement outcomes, we are likely to discover aspects of the relational logic of rural life which will improve our sense of what to measure at the aggregate level. This does not mean that the analysis of entitlement events will be free of statistical, observational, or interpretive challenges. But it does not mean that *any* yield at this level might create a better theoretical basis for aggregative enquiries.

Finally, even if several of these very specific problems can be solved, there remains the challenge of how to use this method in some reasonably rigorous *longitudinal* manner, so that change can systematically be addressed. But this is a second-order challenge which is barely worth worrying about before establishing the viability of this strategy at a lower level of refinement. At the least, this sort of proposal has the virtue of not being just a diplomatic gesture towards better relations between village-level analysts and those working at larger scales.

From Distributions to Relations

I wish now to draw together several strands of the argument and suggestions I have made so far. Specifically, I wish to clarify the link between problems of scale, terminology, relationality, and the measurement of rural economic change. My central claim is that current large-scale approaches to the problem of measuring rural economic change in South Asia need to move from *distributional* to *relational* analyses. That is, they need to cast light not only on net outcomes of social processes, seen largely in measurable bundles of goods and services possessed by households (and individuals) at given points in time. What is systematically not captured in current approaches is the *relational* dimension of the processes which lead to these outcomes. These relational processes, as I have already suggested, involve the ongoing traffic in goods, services, and information between individuals, households, larger corporate groups, and classes. Many aggregate distributive profiles are complex outcomes of ongoing relational processes.

In order to create a better methodological interaction between small-scale relational processes of rural India and large-scale *distributional* profiles, I suggested a strategy (based on the work of Randall Collins), focused on the analysis of entitlement events. The problems of sampling, observer-effect, and aggregation associated with such events are considerable, but may not be insuperable. But the great potential of such an effort would be to illuminate relational processes in a manner that enriches the theoretical basis of aggregate analysis.

My anthropological experience, discussed earlier in this essay, suggests that in order to properly grasp entitlement processes in rural South Asia, we need to be especially sensitive to terminological problems, especially those associated with measurement. In analyzing entitlement events at the small-scale, rural level, efforts at aggregation will fail unless we evolve an honest resolution of the disparity between the linguistic practices associated with the measurement activities of South Asian farmers and those associated with the practice of social science. Central among these is the fact that a good deal of rural talk involves approximation and comparison, whereas our standard social science techniques call for numerical precision and absolute measures. Since farmers often use *comparative* measures while our surveys demand *absolute* measures, our instruments create images of rural economy which are both meaninglessly precise as well as lacking in the comparative approach to magnitude which farmers realize is essential. Of course, these drawbacks in our instruments and approaches are directly based on our larger incapacity to rethink our theoretical bases for aggregate data collection.

Finally, the problem of rural economic change, from the viewpoint of *measurement*, cannot satisfactorily be solved until the prior question of *aggregation* is satisfactorily resolved. My own proposal is addressed principally to the theoretical basis of aggregation without reference to questions of change over time. But it should by now be clear that, in my view, it will neither suffice to (a) keep refining existing statistical techniques for longitudinal analysis or (b) encourage anthropologists to do "re-studies" at the village level. While these are laudable goals in themselves, they do not cut through the current methodological gap between large- and small-scale analyses. Until we develop ways of looking at relational processes at the micro level, and do so in a way that refines aggregation by improving the framework of macro-sociological theory, efforts to measure rural economic change will remain either trivial (because of their non-representativeness) or sterile (because they do not illuminate relationships between actors/social units).

Ecumenism and Epistemology

Since this volume [Bardhan 1989, in which this essay was originally published] does attempt to create a dialogue between anthropologists and economists working on problems of measurement involved in the study of rural change in India, it seems worthwhile to conclude with some thoughts on the nature of the dialogue itself.

From my perspective, there are two sorts of essays in the volume. The first sort, which is "ecumenical" in spirit (and would include the papers by Breman, Harriss, Jodha, Tendulkar, Wadley and Derr, and Vaidyanathan) does not see any fundamental obstacles to a sustained dialogue between the two disciplines, in spite of important differences in methods, assumptions, and goals. These essays see a difference in method as being largely *technical*, and therefore as soluble largely by *technical* innovations and self-criticism on both sides. The second sort, represented by the essays of Bhattacharya and Chattopadhyay, Rudra, Srinivasan, and myself, though written with varying degrees of explicit combativeness, do raise problems that cannot easily be classified as simply technical and, thus, as soluble simply by technical means. Juxtaposing this second set of essays raises a set of issues that I would call *epistemological* rather than *technical*.

In the remainder of my remarks, I shall not deal with the "ecumenical" essays (nor the ecumenical component of the second set of essays) but rather with the essays that raise "epistemological" issues, though some of the authors may vigorously resist this labeling of the problems they raise, as resistance is itself part of the problem. The problems I have in mind are reflected in the various positions taken on matters of "conceptual subjectivity" versus investigator bias (Srinivasan), quantitative versus qualitative approaches (Srinivasan), sampling versus complete enumeration (Rudra), response errors versus non-sampling bias (Bhattacharya and Chattopadhyay), and the issue of relational versus distributional dimensions in the study of rural change (Appadurai). As most of the essays in the volume show, especially the group that I have called "ecumenical," but also most of the essays in the second set, there is a point up to which these issues also can be resolved once they have been recognized, and appropriate methodological steps are taken. But there remains an irreducible component of disagreement, most explicit perhaps in the essays by Srinivasan and myself, but certainly reflected to some degree in all the papers.

This residue of disagreement needs to be brought explicitly, if briefly, into public view in a volume such as this one, so that the debate between methods in the study of rural change in India (or elsewhere) does not become prematurely friendly. At bottom, in my opinion, are not issues about sampling size, respondent error, investigator bias, purposive sampling, etc., though these are important issues about which we all need to be clearer, and in regard to which this volume represents much valuable thought. The deeper issue is *epistemological*, and involves debates about the social scientist (and the effects of his or her methods on the objects of study), a problem which should not appear trivial to anyone familiar with the Heisenberg problem of observer-effect on experiments. Both in the social sciences as well as in the natural sciences, those persons concerned with thinking *about* science, and not just practicing it in the mode of business as usual, are conducting serious debates about what constitutes certainty in science, about the deep problems involved in separating epistemological *conventions* from ontological certainties, and about the relationship between numerical precision and the analysis of living forms, whether these are human or nonhuman.

It would be inappropriate to review this debate. But suffice it to say that we would all be well advised not to pretend that there is some unshakeable and timeless edifice regarding measurement, objectivity, and the status of "facts" and factual error. For those among us who wish to continue the practice of a statistically based social science, where all significant problems of measurement are regarded as either already solved or potentially soluble, I think there might be something to be said for reflecting more carefully about current debates among scientists and philosophers of science before concluding, as Srinivasan provocatively does, that the problem of the relationship between quantitative and qualitative factors is "a phony one." One might mix metaphors here and suggest that the larger desert is a phony problem to the ostrich with his head in the sand. Anthropologists, likewise, will have to worry a lot more about their long-standing fetish concerning "holism," a fetish I have criticized elsewhere (Appadurai 1986b, 1988). Here, my position converges with Rudra's, though the paths taken to our positions may not be identical.

The major questions are: whether problems of social life (and standard of living) can be reduced largely to their quantitative dimensions (and still remain significant); whether the difficulties of grasping even these quantitative dimensions can be further reduced to the technical issues of "bias," "error," and "sampling," as defined and perceived through the lens of statistics; and whether the problems of how rural people talk and think can be divorced from the fact that serious differences of worldview and terminology separate them from the social scientists who study them. I doubt that these differences can be solved simply by more sensitive training of local-level survey administrators, or by more sophisticated use of stratified samples, and better statistical methods for aggregation, although I am all for such improvements. The problems of translation involved here, especially if they are as fundamental as I have argued, raise epistemological questions. Particularly, they raise the question of the degree to which what we want to "know" is "knowable" within the terms of our current apparatus (both of assumptions and of techniques).

To take the route, articulated most forcefully by Srinivasan, that problems (or dimensions of problems) that are not tractable to existing statistical techniques are irrelevant to measurement, and that measurement is the *sine qua non* of social science, is to commence a circular argument. In this argument, a certain idea of "measurement" (itself employed without adequate attention to its epistemological assumptions) is made not merely a technique, but a criterion of what is a "scientific" problem, and then anything which is intractable to this *specific* ideology of measurement is consigned to some nonscientific hell (or heaven). This not only amounts to putting the cart before the horse, it also amounts to making the cart pull the horse, and, if it fails, killing the horse or changing its shape by chopping off a few of its limbs, rather than redesigning the cart. I believe some version of this circular position is quite prevalent, and neither reducing the problem to its technical dimensions nor pretending that goodwill will solve everything is adequate. This volume opens a dialogue which, in my judgment, is most important because it exposes our differences at the level of our ideologies of measurement, of epistemology, and, dare I say it, of "science" itself. Without admitting and addressing this problem, all talk of solutions, including my own, is probably over-optimistic.

Acknowledgments

The fieldwork on which this essay is based was conducted with financial support from the Social Science Research Council, the National Science Foundation, and the American Institute for Indian Studies. The essay was prepared with financial support from the University of Pennsylvania and the Center for Advanced Study in the Behavioral Sciences at Stanford University (through grant BNS-8011494 from the National Science Foundation). In the early stages of conceptualizing the essay I had useful discussions with Ellen Comisso, Paul DiMaggio, Stephen Fienberg, Ulf Hannerz, and Karl Shell, though none of them is responsible for the views expressed here. An earlier version of this paper was presented at a conference on "Rural Economic Change in South Asia" sponsored by the Joint Committee on South Asia of the American Council of Learned Societies and the Social Science Research Council, in Bangalore (India) on August 5–8, 1986. I am grateful to all the participants at the conference for their comments and suggestions, and especially to Pranab Bardhan. Amartya Sen generously commented on an earlier draft and helped me to sharpen several key points.

CHAPTER 3

Wells in Western India: Irrigation and Cooperation in an Agricultural Society

Introduction

The principal purpose of this paper is to describe the social arrangements surrounding access to water from open-surface wells in a rural Indian setting. This description raises certain questions concerning the sociology of cooperation in a traditional agricultural society undergoing rapid economic and technical change. Some of these questions are briefly discussed in the conclusion.

Context

Control over the means of production—land, labor, tools, animals, water, and money—both stratifies and connects rural households in the villages of South Asia. It stratifies them because some of these households invariably control more of these resources than others. It connects them because features of the social organization of production place these households in positions of cooperation with one another. Such features include a variety of forms of joint ownership of land and other resources, formal and informal exchange arrangements for tools and for labor between households, crop-sharing arrangements, legal and illegal uses of land as security in loan transactions, tenancy relations, and sharing systems for water resources. Some of these relations have recently been carefully described by Lee Schlesinger for a village in Satara district, Maharashtra (Schlesinger 1981).

I use the term "cooperation" in this context with some hesitation, for it frequently implies equality between partners and equally cheerful attitudes on both sides. Though this is sometimes the nature of cooperation in situations such as the one I shall describe, more often cooperation is a state of affairs that involves households of different economic capability, and that may not be regarded as especially desirable by some of the parties involved.

This paper uses data collected in 1981–82 from a single village in Maharashtra to consider one form of cooperation, that which is involved in the problem of access to water for agricultural production. By describing the technology, social organization, and political economy of open-surface wells in this village, I hope to cast some light on the very complicated ways in which cooperation is related to the distribution of resources in one kind of agricultural milieu. Villagers do cooperate in other contexts and on other scales. Extended families jointly operate domestic units and sometimes work their plots together. Larger kin units cooperate in bearing the costs and labor needs of large-scale ceremonies, such as those involved in marriages and funerals. Lineages work together to celebrate the festival days of lineage deities. Farmers sometimes have special cooperative arrangements for the sharing of bullocks and related equipment for key agricultural activities. Women form teams that sell their services for specialized agricultural activities, such as the planting of onions. Men form teams that dig wells by contract. All of the households in the village make some contribution to the festival of the principal village deity, and most households have made some financial contribution to the recent renovation of the shrine of this deity. Water from wells, therefore, is not the only interest which draws farmers together in cooperative arrangements. But it is a cooperative context of special complexity and importance.

Before I describe the village I worked in, I should point out that open-surface wells constitute an important feature of this agrarian society for several reasons. First, according to the Season and Crop Report for Maharashtra State for 1975–76, the area under well irrigation was over 60 percent of the net irrigated land of the state, with surface irrigation being used for less than 40 percent. Further, at least in the mid-70s, well-irrigated land was increasing at twice the rate of land under surface irrigation. Also, between 1974–75 and 1975–76 the number of electric pumps on wells increased by 12.5 percent. Maharashtra is very backward in comparison to other states in terms of the amount of irrigated land. It is further clear that wells play a quantitative role in irrigation in Maharashtra which is probably unique in India. In closely examining the social organization and political economy of well irrigation in a Maharashtrian village we are, therefore, looking at a particular aspect of the transformation of the agrarian landscape in India.

Second, and simply from a descriptive point of view, most anthropological accounts of irrigation systems, to my knowledge, deal with spatially and technologically larger ones, i.e., supra-village systems. Brian Spooner's account of qanat systems on the Iranian plateau is among the very few which deal with systems of a comparably small scale (Spooner 1974).

Third, such wells and access to the water in them constitute the critical link between rural production and the market in agricultural commodities in contemporary Maharashtra. By extension, in the particular village discussed here the sale of agricultural commodities grown on plots watered by these wells is the most important source of cash in two senses: for those who can successfully market these products, this is likely to be their most substantial and predictable source of cash; and, this commercialized agriculture is also likely to be the principal source of cash for those men and women who sell their labor to others, either because they are landless or because they have too little land to meet their minimum needs.

Fourth, for technical reasons that will become apparent as I proceed, there is good reason to believe that the current use of these wells represents a major intensification of commercialized agriculture in this region, with certain historical implications and possibilities. For all these reasons, a careful analysis of the political economy of wells in a village in Maharashtra ought to tell us something of value about the changing relations between the forces of commercialization in agriculture and the local organization of rural production.

The Ethnographic Locus

The village from which I have drawn this data— and to which I have given the pseudonym Vadi—is located about 25 miles southeast of the city of Pune, in Purandhar *taluq* (subdivision), Pune district, Maharashtra State. For non-Indianists, this places it in Western India, about

130 miles inland from the coastal metropolis of Mumbai. Its location also places it on a gradient of decreasing rainfall in the Deccan Plateau. Rainfall in Vadi totals probably less than 25 inches in most years, and is sharply seasonal. The peak period of rainfall in normal years is in the months of June, July, August, and September, which account for about 75 percent of this total. October and November usually account for about 15 percent, the months from December to March for about 3 percent, and April and May for about 7 percent. These figures are very approximate, for there can be sharp year-to-year fluctuations from this norm. The village is about 2.5 miles from Saswad, the *taluq* headquarters, which is the principal bus link to Pune and to Mumbai.

There is a road that goes by the village which is used by the buses of the State Transport system and by the trucks of the transport companies that move vegetables from villages like Vadi to Pune and to Mumbai.

The population of Vadi consists of approximately 900 persons, who are distributed in 193 households. About 30 percent of these households contain families that are "joint" (*ekatra*) in one or another sense, while the remaining 70 percent are "nuclear" (*vibhakta*). The total amount of cultivated land is about 880 acres, of which about 280 acres (less than 33 percent) is wet land, i.e., land that has access to water above and beyond rainwater. Mean landholdings are 4.5 acres, with mean dry landholdings being 3.1 acres and mean wet landholdings being 1.4 acres.

Vadi has a very significant set of links with the outside world. Out of the 193 households, 104 have one (and often more) member of the family outside the village, usually earning a living in Mumbai or Pune. But this should not give the impression that Vadi is a "remittance economy" in any simple sense, since many of these wage-earners support dependents in the city, and others, for a variety of reasons, send cash back to the village only in special circumstances. Thus it is no surprise that although 104 households have working members outside Vadi, only 33 of these households described cash salaries as their principal means of subsistence (when compared with income from cash crops, sale of family labor, and the products of their own fields).

The caste composition of Vadi is relatively simple. Out of the total households, 174 are Maratha, and the rest are distributed among the Mahar, Mang, Chambhar, Gurav, Lohar, Nhavi, and Ramoshi castes. When villagers state that this is a "Maratha" village, they are not far wrong. The Maratha households themselves are organized into four numerically dominant lineages (*bhauki*) and three numerically minor ones. The families in each lineage share surnames (*adnav*), although there is here an ethnographic curiosity in that two of the dominant Maratha lineages share the same *ādnāv*. The families of the other castes are similarly identifiable by shared surnames.

I have already noted that mean landholdings are small. Agriculture, to produce crops for both household consumption as well as for sale, is the principal economic activity of the villagers. The principal subsistence crops are sorghum (*jowar*) and millet (*bajri*), and most villagers grow at least some of each. In addition, however, there is a very large inventory of other cultivars. Small amounts of wheat and rice are grown. The principal commercial crops are sugarcane, onions, and green peas. Also important, but more for consumption than for sale, are a variety of lentils and pulses, peanuts, many kinds of greens, and small amounts of tomatoes, carrots, figs, fodder grass, and flowers. All the crops grown principally for sale (and here peas and onions are the most important), as well as the vegetables grown for home consumption, require irrigated land.

There are two major cropping seasons: the *kharif* season, from June to October (which relies on the monsoon rains) and the *rabi* (or winter) season, when the bulk of the irrigation-dependent, market-oriented farming is done, which runs from November to February. The hot (*unhālā*) season from March to May is the most taxing because of the heat and lack of water, but those who do have access to water in this season use it to grow certain vegetables. The hot season is also the season for repair of tools, preparation of the land in anticipation of the June rains, and the celebration of marriage and other village festivities. It is the season of high expenditure and low income for many households.

While the technology of agriculture is largely traditional, its economic framework is no longer so traditional. The bullock and the plow are still the key instruments of agriculture, and the tools used for winnowing, weeding, reaping, sowing, threshing, and harvesting are still largely part of a very ancient material inventory. Yet there have been important changes. The use of fertilizer and of pesticides, particularly for cash crops, has become common, and animal manure is now infrequently used. Agricultural labor is paid for virtually entirely in cash, and there are clearly understood rates of payment for different tasks, seasons, and genders. Vadi is a labor-surplus village, for though there are very few landless households, the number of land-poor households is quite large. Even the intermittent flow of urban remittances is inadequate to sustain the land-poor households, whose women and men must sell their labor in addition to using it to manage their own small holdings. Thus, it is not often that the farmers of Vadi need to hire laborers from other villages.

Vadi is now in a variety of ways deeply monetized. Even the poorest households are deeply tied into the cash nexus and most households, in the opinion of these farmers, would now collapse without a few hundred rupees per month, at the very least (Rs. 9 = US $1 then). One major way to improve one's position in a world dominated by cash transaction is to enter the market in agricultural commodities, not only as a laborer (where the prospects for improvements are dismal) but as a producer. This means gaining access, however precariously, to irrigated land. This is where wells enter the picture.

The Place of Wells in Agrarian Culture

Though my concern in this paper is with some sociological and economic problems raised by the use of wells in Vadi, it should be made clear that to the farmers of Vadi, wells are not usually regarded from an aggregate point of view, nor simply as parts of the capital required for agriculture. There are now 74 wells (*vihīr*) in Vadi and most of them are seen as individual entities, with names, histories, and idiosyncrasies. Wells are part of the known landscape of the village, and they serve to demarcate the landscape at the same time as they derive their own distinctiveness from it. Their names sometimes refer to the fields in which they lie, and these field names, like all traditional toponyms, contain the memory of previous owners of the soil, reflect qualities of the soil in the vicinity, or serve as reminders of the lineages controlling that soil, or of particular fruits or crops for which the land associated with the well is known. Not all of the names have folk explanations, but most are associated with shared knowledge of features of the history, landscape, and social framework of the well in question.

Space and time come together in the names of these wells, although not all farmers know all there is to be known about these names. What is known is a good deal about who now are the sharers in the well, when it was built, its reputation for being a plentiful source of water (or not). Given the number of wells, and the complexities of the system of sharing in them, such knowledge is not evenly shared and is sometimes out of date. Well water, like all water, is believed to contain deified powers, and when new wells are inaugurated, there is a special ritual offering to these divinities, in which representations of fertility and auspiciousness are central. Wells thus form a very important part of the human landscape of Vadi, and it is the willingness of farmers to talk in detail and at length about the wells in which they have shares that has made possible the discussion that follows.

The Technology of Wells

The basic technological structure of the 74 wells currently in use in Vadi probably goes back at least a millennium and consists of a hole dug in the soil to a depth of anywhere from 20 to 60 feet, and with a diameter of anywhere from 15 to 30 feet. The traditional measure for the depth of a well is a *paras* or *purush*, indicating the height of an adult male but actually equivalent to about 7 feet. Although some wells were probably dug by family or village labor, specialist castes of well-diggers are a well-known part of the historical record in western and southern India. In the past, the inner walls of this hole might be "finished" with stone and lime, and there would have been a wooden superstructure. This superstructure would permit the dropping and lifting of a leather water container. The raising and lifting would have been accomplished either by two or four bullocks.

Today, wells have acquired some new features, though they are fundamentally unchanged. Cement has largely replaced lime for the finishing of the interior; steel containers (*mōt*) have replaced the leather water containers; and, in a few cases, rented boring machines have replaced human labor for the actual digging. Most important, animal power is now regarded as obsolete, although about 12 wells still use this form of power. The energy source of choice is electricity, although about 5 wells are powered by oil engines. This means that there are today about 57 wells that are powered by 3 or 5 hp electric motors. Sometimes these modernized wells have varying lengths of pipeline, but often traditional dug channels (*pāt*) are used to take the water from the mouth of the well to the fields. Most wells physically predate the arrival of electricity, and are thus simply electrified traditional open-surface wells. The technology of wells may thus better be called mixed than traditional.

Another aspect of the technology of wells is mixed, and that is the technique by which decisions are made about where the well should be located. Farmers tend to rely on the prognostications of specialists called *pānhādi* (water-diviner), who are men and women with other regular occupations but who are known to have a talent for spotting subsurface water. These diviners suggest not only locations for digging but also offer predictions about the depth at which water is likely to be struck and the nature of the soil likely to be encountered. Given the massive investment that new wells represent, farmers tend to consult more than one diviner, sometimes a government geological expert, and finally triangulate these expert suggestions with their own knowledge about the likely location of subsurface veins based on their assessment of the relative productivity of other wells in the vicinity.

The Distribution and Control of Wells

Wells are part of the picture of very small and fragmented holdings in Vadi, but are also indicative of a relatively high proportion (33 percent) of irrigated land to total cultivated land, compared to the figure for the state, which was 11 percent in 1975–76. In Vadi, 142 households share about 280 acres of wet land. Of these households, about 33 percent have wet landholdings of less than 1 acre, about 60 percent have less than 2 acres, and about 80 percent have less than 3 acres. Only 11 of these households have more than 5 irrigated acres each, and 1 of these has 25 acres which is the largest concentration of wet landholdings in Vadi. I present these figures to show that these irrigated holdings are extremely modest, by and large.

Most farmers own several plots (*tukdē*) of wet land; these holdings are not usually physically contiguous, which means that the farmers are often shareholders (*hissēdār, vātēkāri*) in more than one well. Although there are 24 single-owner wells, and 13 two-owner wells, even the farmers involved in these have shares in some of the other wells, which have co-sharers ranging in number from 3 to the most involuted case, which has 31 co-sharers. The scattered picture of individual landholdings is further layered over by a crisscrossing web of shares in wells. Shares in wells usually remain attached to the pieces of land with which they are associated and, in Vadi, to buy or inherit a piece of land is by definition to inherit a share in the well which allows it to be irrigated. Yet shares in wells are not entirely tied to pieces of land, for wells can fall into disuse, or water from one well (theoretically meant to irrigate a particular plot) can be diverted by the shareholder to another plot not associated with it, or well shares can lie dormant while the pieces of land associated with them may be watered by water from another well to which the shareholder has access.

Nevertheless, as a rule, shares in wells are closely associated with pieces of land, and thus the major way in which current shareholders in wells acquire these holdings is through land inherited from their male parents. This is reflected in the fact that many wells have shareholders who are all male agnates (paternal kinsmen) from the same named lineage, and sometimes they might be sons of the same father. This picture of patrilineally inherited shares is fairly persistent, so that when one encounters a well which has mixed lineage membership, or in which there is one anomalous surname, it can easily be traced to one of the following three sources: a sale of the land (and the associated well share) to an outsider by a lineage member in financial difficulty; the acquisition of a piece of lineage land by an outsider because of a loan default in which the land was the security (*tāran*); or, in the few cases where a woman is named as a shareholder, it turns out that she is a widowed member of the lineage, whose husband received the land as part of her dowry, and the land has reverted to her after his death.

Turn-Taking and Constraints on Production

Approximately 33 percent of these wells have between 1 and 4 shareholders and thus do not require complex systems for sharing water. But the remaining 66 percent, which have between 5 and 31 shareholders, do require complex time-sharing systems. To understand these systems, it is necessary to have some background concerning the role of wells in agricultural production. Well-watered land is crucial to growing most crops in the winter and summer seasons when the rains are minimal. Very few wells have water through all 12 months, and it is these few 12-month wells (*bārāmāhi*) that allow their beneficiaries to grow sugarcane, which requires ample water throughout the year. The bulk of wells are known as 8-month wells (*ātmāhi*), and yield water from approximately mid-June to mid-February. Such 8-month wells permit the growing of onions and green peas (the two major cash crops), plus a variety of other vegetables and fruits which are grown both for market and for home consumption, as well as small amounts of rice and wheat.

In wells that have more than four or five shareholders, who are working small plots of land and growing the same cash crops (such as onions) at much the same times, there are fairly complex turn-taking (*pāli*) systems. These systems vary depending on the number of shareholders, the water retention capabilities of the well, especially in the hot weather, the crops being grown by the shareholders, and the amount of land under the well in question. Usually the system is a 12-day or 8-day rotation, and the amount of time (1 day or 2 days or a part of a day) that a particular turn consists of depends on the amount of land that a particular landholder has in his share. It is in the hot season, when the water level drops, and when the cash crops need water in order to yield profits, that these systems come into play. It is also at these times that those farmers who have access to their own wells, or to low-membership wells, have the greatest advantage.

In general, partly because of the fragmented holdings under wells and the problem of low capital for many of these farmers, few wells involve 100 percent use of the plots that are described as being "under" them (*vihīrīkhāli*). Frequently only a third of the acreage nominally associated with the well is actually in productive use. This is a sign of the incapacity of shareholders to afford the labor and other costs associated with full use of their well-linked acreage. In most cases, the underutilization of these nominally irrigated plots is a function of these disabilities and not of the limits of the wells alone. Consolidation of holdings is the key to the economics of using these wells optimally, but most farmers have holdings that are far from each other in addition to being small. Wealthier farmers are always seeking to acquire, either by direct purchase or by mortgage defaults, plots near ones they already own.

All farmers in Vadi who lack access to shares in wells would like to acquire such shares. All farmers with shares would like to see these shares electrified. (I speak of electrified "shares" rather than of electrified wells because there are several cases of wells in which some shareholders have invested in motors which they operate during their turns. The motor is not available to other shareholders who could not afford to participate in the original investment, and who therefore use bullock power during their turns or, in a few cases, rent oil engines which are portable.) And all farmers would like to have wells of their own, preferably electrified, without having to cooperate with other farmers in the original investment or in the subsequent turn-taking.

The motorized wells which have multiple shareholders clearly reflect the fact that the costs of electrification (a 3 hp motor costs about Rs. 5000 [$555] and a 5 hp motor about Rs. 8000) are beyond the reach of most farmers. Yet, the decision to invest jointly in a new well is even harder than the decision to invest jointly in a new motor for an existing well. The costs of a new well, including digging it, installing a motor, and perhaps installing pipeline, can go from Rs. 20,000 ($2222) to Rs. 40,000. This is a very sizable investment, since the mean annual cash income of most small farmers (from all sources) is unlikely to exceed

Rs. 5000. Given the small individual plots, the chances that some of the co-sharers will not be able to afford the inputs to make the optimal use of the irrigated land, and the chances that economic difficulties will make some of them renege on their share of the bank loan repayments or the electricity bills, it is no surprise that all but one of the new wells dug in the last five years are entrepreneurial ventures by single farmers. There have been joint efforts to electrify existing wells, but there are several wells where plans to electrify have not come to fruition, and others that, though electrified, are underutilized, especially by the poorer shareholders.

Sharing and Conflict

Though current sharing systems in the multi-shareholder wells are quite involuted, they are surprisingly conflict-free. Problems do arise, and these come from a variety of sources: most common is the usurpation of part of another shareholder's turn; using the water from a turn to water land which is not attached to the relevant well but to another one; or the incapacity or refusal of a shareholder to participate in repair costs, electricity costs, or the costs of repaying bank loans. Perhaps the most frequent source of tension is the question of what happens to a turn disrupted by a failure in the electricity supply or by a breakdown in the motor. Most well-sharers have agreed that the fair solution is to allow the turn to resume, rather than to lapse, after the problem is solved. It is not at all obvious, furthermore, that tension appears to increase with the number of shareholders or the overall intensity of use. There is, however, a definite seasonality to tension around wells, with the hot season being the fragile temporal zone. The largest number of shareholders is associated with a particular lineage, 31 of whom use a certain well, involving a very complex and involuted system of turns. But this is a very disciplined and well-managed lineage, which, in this as in other matters, is very good at handling internal problems effectively and quickly.

In general, it seems as if the family and lineage basis of these groupings has a good deal to do with the low level of conflict occurring in them, not because families and lineages are interpersonal utopias, but because *as long as a group of agnates maintains its productive interests jointly,* they have a variety of emotional, social, and corporate reasons to resolve conflict rapidly. In these cases, as well as in those that involve non-related farmers, the other factor that preempts complete disruption of the system is the shared awareness that a complete breakdown is simply too costly for all concerned, given the short commercial cropping season, the high costs of the inputs, and the need to get maximum yields in order not to face significant financial losses. Indeed, in the case of the bulk of the multi-owner wells, the fact that these are small farmers holding on to the commodity market with very small margins for failure makes them less prone to pursue disputes in ways that bigger landowners can afford, in this and other parts of South Asia. Disputes about "honor," such as Douglas Merrey has reported in the large-scale irrigation systems of Pakistani Punjab (Merrey 1983), might require a larger size of holding, before they become chronic and endemic.

Wells, Commercialization, and Cooperation

Looking at the state as a whole, it is clear that irrigation, and the commercialized agriculture it supports, is the basis of a dominant peasant class economy. These rural villagers use modern forms of capital (including cash) in a massive way in agriculture, and generate significant profits from the sale of agricultural commodities. The technology of well irrigation plays an unusually important role in supporting this development in contemporary Maharashtra, as I have already suggested. Further, the electrification of these wells, which is clearly proceeding rapidly, is a new technical means to intensify commodity production in agriculture. Given the small amount of irrigated land in the state, this suggests the rapid formation of a small class of capitalist farmers who consume the labor of other, less wealthy farmers, and reap the bulk of the profits from commercialization. From the village perspective, at least in cases such as Vadi, the picture is more complex, for irrigated land is spread among a very large number of households. Thus, though a few of these families constitute a truly distinct category in terms of their sole ownership of wells and the relatively large amounts of wet land they own (as well as certain other endowments that I have not discussed here), on the whole, irrigated plots are part of the precarious struggle to survive and reproduce of a large number of small farming households, who do not form a wealthy class in any obvious way.

For these smaller farmers, cooperation in complex water-sharing systems is apparently a function of both the costs and the rewards of commercialized agriculture based on the availability of electricity. Such cooperation is not regarded as either desirable in itself or as optimal, and most farmers are perfectly clear that they would prefer independent ownership of wells. But cooperation is, for most farmers, the only way to gain some access to the benefits of commercialized agriculture, and is, at the same time, a way to retain some independence from the market for meeting their own consumption requirements in certain vegetables and grains. It must also be stressed, however, that the traditional structures for organizing such cooperation, which are kin-centered even if not completely kin-based, are remarkably effective and conflict-free. From the point of view of the actors, such cooperation is largely a result of the disciplined effort of small farmers to gain access to those resources which they hope will permit them to become free (as producers) of those very structures of kinship, inheritance, and sharing on which such cooperation is currently based. Farmers cooperate in the short run so that, if they are fortunate, they may not have to do so in the long run. This orientation to the possibility of autonomy from collective forms of organization may be the single most important result of intensified access to cash incomes, electricity, and urban markets.

Acknowledgments

Earlier versions of this paper were presented at the panel on "Rethinking Agricultural Research for South and Southwest Asia," Annual Meeting of Mid-Atlantic Region of the Association of Asian Studies, October 28–30, 1983, Philadelphia, PA, and the First International Conference on Maharashtra, University of Toronto, March 18–20, 1984. I am grateful to participants in each of these gatherings for their critical comments and suggestions. For comments on earlier written and oral versions, I am especially grateful to Sandra Barnes, Robert Hunt, Douglas Merrey, Loren Michael, Brian Spooner, and Bernard Wailes.

The fieldwork on which this paper is based was conducted in 1981–82 with financial support from the National Science Foundation, the American Institute of Indian Studies, the Joint Committee on South Asia of the ACLS/SSRC. Dipak Kumbharkar and Devidas Tarwade assisted in the collection of the data in the field. A grant from the University Research Foundation, University of Pennsylvania, aided in the analysis of some of the data.

CHAPTER 4

Dietary Improvisation in an Agricultural Economy

This chapter treats decisions concerning food in the domestic settings of an Indian village as examples of what Pierre Bourdieu has called the "regulated improvisations of the habitus" (Bourdieu 1977: 21). This means that such decisions are not best regarded either as the mechanical products of consciously held "rules" or as ad hoc and culture-free responses to raw exigency. Rather, they are culturally formed dispositions to strategize in particular ways. I will make three kinds of observation and an argument about their interconnectedness. The first concerns the relationship between the taken-for-granted aspects of decision-making in a particular cultural and economic setting and those that are more in the foreground of attention (Schutz 1970). The second observation concerns the relationship between dietary decisions and other kinds of preoccupation in the daily lives of adult female household heads. The third deals with the highly permeable boundaries (both analytic and practical) between the domestic setting and the more public, large-scale factors that affect the political economy of the hearth. Though my information comes from a particular social, cultural, and historical milieu, I am quite aware that what it describes is a variant of the sort of predicament in which women find themselves in a wide variety of societies.[1]

---

1. Since there are very few citations in the text of this chapter, I should note that I have been influenced, in a variety of ways, by the following scholars and studies. On the status of working women in India, I have learned a

Some Dilemmas of Description

Self-consciousness about one's mode of presentation has recently become something of a fashion among ethnographers, following upon an earlier tendency to scrutinize the epistemological dilemmas of fieldwork. Since this chapter is written in a manner that does not fit standard modes of exposition in the study of dietary decision-making, its own rhetorical stance is worth justifying.

My goal is to highlight certain qualitative, subjective, and experiential aspects of day-to-day subsistence in a particular place. I have therefore deliberately minimized the presentation of quantities, objective structures, and rules, except insofar as they illuminate the experiential side of the picture. Though I cannot provide a full justification here, my position is built on the critique of "objectivism" in Bourdieu (1977) and of standard social science modes of measurement in Cicourel (1964) and Appadurai (1984b [see chapter 1, this volume]). I am aware that this endangers the credibility of my argument for some readers, but this seems to me preferable to dangers of the other sort.

Even if my qualitative emphasis is taken to be legitimate, it might be argued that my account is thin on actual vignettes or cases, which are often held to be the bases of descriptive ethnography. I have opted instead for a type of generalizing rhetoric, which glosses and represents cases. There is a reason for this choice as well, beyond limitations of space. Just as certain kinds of objectivist account exaggerate the significance of "rule," "structure," and "determinacy" in human action, so certain qualitative accounts, through excessive reliance on vignettes, cases, and "real" examples, create the problematic (and misleading) illusion that lived experience always has a dramatistic quality—that it is character-centered, unpredictable, and situation-based. This dramatistic illusion is, except for occasional episodes, untrue both to how most people experience their lives and to how anthropologists piece together their understandings in the field. I have therefore opted for a narrative

---

great deal from Gulati (1981), Miller (1981), Papanek (1979, 1984), and Sharma (1980). N. S. Jodha's numerous microlevel analyses of agriculture in semiarid environments in India have provided suggestive descriptions and hypotheses (see, e.g., Jodha 1980, 1986, 1989). Chambers, Longhurst, and Pacey (1981) made me aware of the complexities of seasonality. Finally, my approach to human action, social forms. and lived experience owes a great deal to Bourdieu (especially Bourdieu 1977) and to Schutz (particularly Schutz 1970).

voice that is simultaneously experiential and synoptic, and thus reflects, in a specific setting, both the typicality of experience and the experience of typicality. The ethnographic account that follows, therefore, is part of an effort to typicalize lived experience without necessarily either generalizing from, or idealizing, actual cases. Much traditional ethnography, of course, typicalizes in this way (see Marcus and Cushman 1982), but it is not so traditional to typicalize when the focus is on the qualitative side of lived experiences. In this specific regard, my effort is experimental.

One final question remains about the idiom in which I have presented this typicalizing account. Although I am concerned in some sense with the mental side of subsistence experience, I have deliberately eschewed the idioms of rational choice, of information processing, and of psychological formalisms of any sort. Instead, I have opted for a phenomenological idiom. This choice too is not simply a matter of taste. In the course of my own fieldwork, I became firmly convinced that the search for mental calculi in the heads of my informants, even if these existed, was methodologically misguided. In the face of situations of immense intricacy, fluidity, and complexity; of responses of great subtlety and speed; and of justifications that are very difficult (even for the participants) to distinguish from motives, the anthropological task of describing the sheer experience of such situations is difficult enough. The search for deeper rules, algorithms, and heuristics seems, at the least, premature. Nevertheless, I do not intend to claim that my type of account is somehow uniquely privileged or authoritative. Indeed, it is partly in the hope of raising some interesting questions for those who are committed to other modes of inquiry and to other strategies of presentation that the following account is offered.

The Village of Vadi

Vadi is my pseudonym for the village in Western India where I conducted fieldwork in 1981–82. This place is located about 25 miles southeast of the city of Pune, in the state of Maharashtra; it is about 130 miles inland (and about a four-hour train ride) from the coastal metropolis of Mumbai. Vadi is a poor village by virtually any standard. It consists of about nine hundred persons who live in 193 households; approximately 30 percent are "nuclear" *(vibhakta),* while the rest are "joint" *(ēkatra)* in one or another sense.[2] The total amount of cultivated land is about 880 acres, of which about 280 acres (less than 33 percent) are irrigated, largely by shared electrically powered wells (Appadurai 1984c [chapter 3 in this volume]). Mean landholdings are 4.5 acres, with mean dry landholdings being 3.1 acres and mean wet landholdings 1.4 acres.

The caste composition of Vadi is not complex. Of the 193 households, 174 belong to the Maratha caste (the dominant peasant caste of this region), while the remaining 19 households are distributed among seven other castes, including two "untouchable" castes. Vadi is the kind of village that in India and elsewhere contributes massively to urban work forces, and 104 of its households have one or more members living outside the village, either in Mumbai or in Pune. The adult males among these migrants often support children and aged adults in their own urban households and thus cannot often send substantial or regular amounts of cash to their families in the village. Vadi is thus not in any simple sense a "remittance economy," though it is in a variety of ways deeply monetized.

Even the poorest of households is fundamentally tied into the cash nexus, and most households, according to widely shared local estimates, would collapse without at least a few hundred rupees a month. Apart from urban remittances, the principal sources of cash are the sale of one's own labor to others in the village and the sale of commercial crops. As for household consumption, few are self-sufficient, even in grain, and

---

2.   Rural speakers of Marathi have a clear lexical way to distinguish "household" *(ghar)* from "family" *(kutumb).* The term *ghar* is, pragmatically speaking, used to refer to the physical dwelling (house); the group of people living together in it; and to domestic aspects of life as opposed to public ones, as in *ghar-kam* (house-work). *Kutumb* is, by contrast, a technical term that is not often used except in formal interview situations, normally to refer to an agnatically related and coresident group of kinsmen with a living male head. But when livelihood is a shared concern among a group of persons, however complex or indirect their kinship links, the term *ghar* (household) is likely to be used. When referring to co-members of a household, who live in separate houses (as when men are away in Mumbai), *ghar* may or may not be used, depending on whether the pragmatic emphasis is on physical dwellings or on budgetary units. Finally, the terms *ēkatra* (united) or *vibhakta* (separate) refer to the commensal and productive relations of agnates, not to physical dwellings: thus, a household with loci in Mumbai and Vadi may nevertheless be a "joint" family *(ēkatra kutumb).*

most rely on village and town shops for vegetables, spices, condiments, cooking oils, clothing, kerosene, matches, and cooking vessels. Even the wealthiest households buy some part of their grain and lentils from the market. On the other hand, there is considerable effort to strive for independence from the market in regard to food, whenever possible.

Agricultural Livelihood

But for a few virtually destitute men and women, who depend entirely on the goodwill of others for their subsistence, all the households in Vadi rely either wholly or in part on agriculture in order to subsist. Agriculture in this part of the Deccan plateau is both a low technology and a high-risk enterprise. Apart from the approximately fifty-seven wells that are powered by small electric or diesel motors, the technology of agriculture relies on animal traction, human labor, and wooden and steel tools that have probably changed in the last few centuries, but only in matters of detail. Modern fertilizers and pesticides are increasingly used for commercial crops, particularly vegetables. Rainfall in Vadi is probably less than twenty-five inches in most years and is sharply seasonal. The peak period of rainfall in normal years is during June, July, August, and September, which accounts for about 75 percent of the total. October and November usually account for about 15 percent, the months from December to March for about 3 percent, and April and May for about 7 percent.

The principal subsistence crops are sorghum *(jowar)* and millet *(bajri)*, and most villagers grow at least some of each. In addition, there is a large inventory of other cultigens. Small amounts of wheat and rice are grown. The principal commercial crops are onions, green peas, sugarcane, and fresh coriander. Also important, but more for consumption than for sale, are a variety of lentils and pulses, many kinds of greens, a few fruits, some oilseeds, and such vegetables as tomatoes, green chilies, garlic, and carrots. Finally, a few farmers devote small parts of their plots to animal fodder. All the crops grown principally for sale, as well as all the vegetables, require irrigated land.

There are two major cropping seasons: the *kharif* season, from June to October (which relies on the monsoon rains), when both sorghum and millet are grown; and the *rabi* (winter) season, which runs from November to January, when the bulk of the irrigation dependent, market-oriented farming is done. The hot season, which runs from March to

May, is the most taxing, because wells run dry, harvests of grain and vegetables have been depleted either through consumption or sale, and expenses for rituals (especially marriages) tend to peak. It is during this hot season that the ritual and the production years reach their highest (followed by their lowest) points of intensity. In May, the ritual cycle subsides, the land is prepared for the following year, and the yearning for the June rains deepens.

Women and the Provision of Food

Food is a subject of special salience in the Hindu world. Since this chapter focuses on the improvisational aspects of domestic subsistence, I shall say something about food as a culturally organized domain of significance in Hindu India. Much of great value has been written on this topic (Marriott 1968, 1976; R. Khare 1976; Stone 1978), and there is surely no need for yet another demonstration that food is part of specialized moral and medical taxonomies; that it ties together ideas of impurity, exchange, and rank; that the logic of the hearth is the logic of the Hindu cosmos in miniature; or that there is a symbolic dimension to food production and processing. Much of this is true for Vadi, though only some of the ways in which these cultural assumptions take shape in the village are addressed in this chapter. In my own previous work, I have sought to contextualize these kinds of significance in problems of micropolitics (Appadurai 1981), of large-scale cultural change (Appadurai 1984b [see chapter 1, this volume]), and of the political economy of entitlement (Appadurai 1984a) in India. What we do need are better accounts of the ways in which these significances are parts of lived local experience, of specific forms of sociality, and of regular improvisatory practice. It is to the latter need that this chapter is addressed.

Throughout my discussion, the problem of domestic food provision is viewed from the female perspective. But a word of clarification is in order. The women of Vadi are neither economically nor existentially in identical situations. Some rely more than others on selling their own agricultural labor. Some have husbands and sons with them, while others head their village households because their husbands are away in Mumbai or Pune. Some are actively involved in farming on their plots, while others, either because they are landless or because they come from larger or wealthier households, do not labor in the fields. Some work under the eye of older women (mothers and mothers-in-law), while others are on their own. Finally, some are too young to bear household responsibilities, while others, because they are poor, infirm, or indifferent, play no role in household decisions. These are important differences, and a full examination would take them carefully into account. But many women are involved in the management of households, rely on produce from their fields as well as on income from the sale of cash crops and their own labor, and are perpetually in one or another form of debt. These are the women—ranging in age from twenty to sixty, all from the dominant Maratha caste, and whose households do not have more than five acres of land—whose voices inform this chapter. Even among them there are important differences, such as the presence or absence of their husbands, the number and health of their children, the age and demands of their parents or in-laws, the prospects for marriage of their sons and daughters, and their own physical strength and health in relation to agricultural labor. Yet, these women have enough in common for my purposes. The resources on which they draw, the problems they face, the language and style of their narratives of their lives, the approach they take to juggling the claims upon them, are similar enough to justify the lumping that must inevitably occur in such an analysis as this one.[3]

Providing food for the daily needs of the household is a responsibility that falls on the shoulders of women in Vadi, but it is a task that is not defined by rigid conceptions or measures of "need" or "requirement." Rather, it is framed by the interaction between a variety of seasonalities and periodicities as they are perceived and engaged in by particular female food providers. Some of these periodicities represent collective, large-scale, and socially set rhythms, such as the cycle of the seasons; the life cycle of specific cultigens; the ups and downs of the labor market; the vagaries of price in the vegetable markets of Saswad (the small market and administrative town about three miles from Vadi), Pune, and Mumbai; and the rhythm of regional, village, and lineage festivals and

---

3.   The data for this chapter come from informal observations and conversations, as well as taped interviews, with women in about twenty households in Vadi. I owe a special debt to Mrs. S. Gogate, my assistant, whose rapport with some of these women helped me to grasp things I would never have understood otherwise. But it is to the women themselves, who improvise domestic security in extremely trying circumstances, that this chapter is dedicated.

rituals. Other periodicities are centripetal and involve trajectories that are idiosyncratic and variable from household to household—marriages and deaths, with their attendant high expenses for ritual; medical emergencies, small and large; cash flows from urban wages, vegetable sales, or sales of labor, which vary not just because of market factors but also in relation to individual energies and choices; biographical periodicities that affect the medical, ritual, and educational needs of children, adult dependents, and adult workers in the household; the complex periodicities of debts, small and large, to banks, vegetable wholesalers, potential affines, neighbors, and kinsmen; and so forth.

In the context of all these periodicities and seasonalities, the struggle to feed members of the household adequately involves the continuous effort to improvise acceptable allocations of time, energy, and money against contextually defined ideas of maternal concern, social standing, and moral propriety. It is the experiential texture of this continuous effort that I wish to capture, at least in part, in the rest of this chapter.

The provision of food in this context entails the juggling of available items (itself a function of the agricultural seasons and of the availability of cash for purchases when necessary) against routine and not-so-routine demands, within the framework of a basic stock of knowledge about food purchasing, processing, cooking, and eating. This knowledge is widely shared as regards recipes; rituals; the needs of the sick, the pregnant, the aged; the shifting prices of foodstuffs; and so on. It is necessarily less shared or standardized in regard to such centripetal and individual factors as individual tastes and income flows. Indeed, it might even be appropriate to call this latter sort of knowledge "information" and reserve the term "knowledge" for the former, shared elements.[4]

---

4. In distinguishing "knowledge" from "information," I wish to contrast two ways in which actors apprehend their environments. While knowledge has to do with retrospect, with regularity, with structure, with generalizations, and with the taken-for-granted, information involves prospect, irregularity, events, particulars, and conscious attention. From the point of view of cultural and social sharing, knowledge is what one has (or thinks one has), whereas information is what one seeks. A full anthropological account of these two categories would be very complex and would, among other things, note that it is within particular frameworks of knowledge that the nature of information itself is defined.

The Structure of the Diet

Against this backdrop, the structure of the diet may be described as *modular, stratified,* and *seasonal.* Let me explain these terms and use them to provide the material context for the strategies of domestic food provision. The building blocks of daily meals are millet- or sorghum-based pan-roasted bread (*bhakri*), an item so basic that its name provides the colloquial term for food; seasonally available vegetables, principally eggplant, onions, garlic, and a variety of greens; soups made of either farm-grown or store-bought lentils of several sorts, principally yellow split peas (*harbara*); seasonings that are themselves used in various standard combinations (these include fresh ingredients, such as coconut, coriander, garlic, red or green chilies, and mustard seed, with vegetable oils as their base); chickpea flour, which has almost the status of a staple; and various hot preserves (*chatni*) made principally of garlic and red chilies. These constitute the modular basis of meals.

Playing a less important role, because they are used either in very small quantities or too occasionally, are meat (usually mutton); fish; chicken; eggs (from household hens); milk (usually from domestic goats, but also from cows and buffaloes); and a variety of sweet, festive preparations whose base is rice, sugar, milk, wheat, chickpea flour, and shortening or clarified butter in various combinations that are both labor and money intensive. Also in a category of their own are tea and sugar, the constant accompaniments of any kind of social activity (sometimes used with milk). Finally, some men (and a few women) smoke *bidis* (native cigarettes), and many women chew a mild narcotic called *mishri*, which is held to be a stimulant and an appetite depressant. These latter items are comestibles but hardly foods. Children, whenever possible, purchase biscuits, toffee, candies, and savories from the two village stores, as do adults less frequently. Children and adults get small quantities of some fruit (mangoes, figs, oranges, bananas), subject to heavy seasonal and wealth variations.

These sets of foods may be described as modular because they represent a group of elements that can be combined into daily, weekly, monthly, and seasonal patterns that are either complex (and therefore both satisfying and nutritious, as far as I can judge) or exceedingly spare and simple. The elementary meal is a few pieces of sorghum or millet bread (*bhakri*) with an extremely hot, concentrated, but cheaply produced *chatni*, usually made of just garlic and red chilies with salt and water. The term used for food, especially by men and women living very close to the bone, is *bhakar-chatni*, referring to just this combination. Other elements can be added progressively to make meals of increasing richness and range. Thus a decent midday meal, especially for working men and women, would include several large pieces of bread, a lentil soup *(amti* or *varan)*, a pan-fried vegetable, and some spicy pickle or condiment. The vegetable and soup items can be made with more or less elaborate spice combinations, and they can be heavy on water and cheap spices or on oil and expensive ones. In the fields, however, most meals consist of just bread and one substantial accompaniment. The most important component of certain routine snack foods is tapioca *(sabudana)*, which is also used on "fast" days. Peanuts play a central role in many vegetable or lentil preparations, and I suspect they are the most reliable sources of protein in the diet in Vadi.

The inventory of foods is also stratified insofar as there is an ordering of the modules, which is fairly explicit. The millet breads form the base (regular, plain, low-cost), along with the chickpea flour-based preparation and *chatnis*. The vegetable and lentil preparations constitute the second tier (with an internal subhierarchy based on the complexity of spices used in them). The top tier is based on animal protein and such high-fat and high-calorie items as meat, sweets, milk products, and eggs. This part of the hierarchy is based on what are regarded as appropriate foods for important ritual events, such as marriages, funerals, and offerings to deities. (More shall be said about feasting in another part of this chapter.) The point about stratification is that it links the modules both to seasonal variation and to stratification in the social sense, since the wealthier households more frequently have combinations of modules involving higher-ranked foodstuffs and preparations.

Seasonality is the most obvious part of this dietary structure. The basic grains are harvested at different times: millet mainly in the *kharif* season, sorghum in both the *kharif* and *rabi* seasons, wheat only in the winter season, and rice at the end of the wet season. The end of the winter and the beginning of the hot season is when the range of vegetables is greatest, because of the irrigation factor, which determines when onions, peas, eggplant, and chilies may be harvested. Lentils and peanuts, because of their preservability, are available on the market throughout the year, as are the basic food grains, spices, oils, flours, salt, and sugar. But for those whose cash income is small and unpredictable, and whose own holdings are tiny and unproductive, foods on the market are not always within their grasp to even out the seasonalities of their own production and the gaps between the harvests of basic grains, as well as between those of vegetables and lentils. These gaps, which occur often at times of greatest need, are closed by contracting short- or long-term debts.

The modular, stratified, and seasonal aspects of the dietary process are deeply interconnected in the experience of the women who are responsible for domestic subsistence in Vadi. The combination of modules into low- and high-quality meals is not only a function of the rank of the modules that are used but also of the seasonalities bearing on the household in question. Festive meals require high-ranking foods and complex modular combinations insofar as the household in question is able to produce them under seasonal constraints. Even ordinary daily meals, whether served at home or in the fields, can be based on very elementary modules or can be complex combinations, depending on the seasonal state of the household in question. There is no set number of meals in the day for a given household. Frequency varies across households (depending on who works and at what distance from home, as well as on the many other factors already mentioned) and within households, where there is a definite tendency to provide multiple, complex, high-ranking food combinations (as far as possible) to workers over nonworkers, to men over women, and to children over nonworking adults. As far as I can see, these latter three criteria are ranked as I have listed them, though a variety of contingencies (such as illness, domestic violence, or the appearance of important guests) may change their ordering.

Let us now move back from the components of the dietary structure to the larger context of women's lives. Women in Vadi stand at the interface between the production and the consumption processes as far as food is concerned. They are actively involved in a large range of agricultural tasks, either in their own fields or, for cash wages, in the fields of others. These tasks include weeding a variety of crops, which is spread through the rainy and winter seasons; planting most of the vegetable crops; harvesting the grain crops and the vegetable crops; and threshing, winnowing, husking, drying, and storing all the cultigens. In addition, they are responsible for the care of the smaller domestic animals (goats and chickens). They do some of the local selling of vegetable and grain surpluses and much of the shopping at the village store. Women whose husbands are away are responsible for monitoring any sharecropping arrangement that they might have for their own plots, which often includes giving their own labor at key times. Finally, and not least, they must get water for domestic use from wells or streams, wash clothes and utensils, collect firewood or manure for fuel, and tend all dependent children. Somewhere in the midst of all these tasks, most of which have irregular and uncertain periodicities, they must think about feeding the members of their households. The experiential quality of this dietary dimension of their daily responsibilities can best be discussed under two headings, which occupy the following two sections of this chapter. These sections also refine, qualify, and contextualize some of the observations made so far.

Scale, Intricacy, and Frequency in Women's Transactions

One implication of the kind of situation that has been sketched thus far is that the nature of tasks, decisions, and transactions in which women in Vadi are engaged is distinctive. This characteristic quality, which has to do with the special *scale*, *intricacy*, and *frequency* of their interactions, is what most distinguishes their situation from that of adult men in comparable households. These are distinct but interrelated qualities, and I deal with them sequentially, starting with scale.

Although there are few areas of subsistence in which women do not have some role, they are typically involved in smaller-scale issues than their husbands, fathers, and sons. This can be seen in a variety of dimensions. Take the matter of money. Typically, women do not handle large sums, either because the money is doled out in small (often unpredictable) amounts by their wage-earning husbands or sons or because they themselves are rarely involved in larger-scale payments for their own labor, usually being paid by the day for most of the work they do. This is true for their agricultural labor (such as weeding, planting, or threshing) and for the domestic chores they sometimes do for other women in the village, such as plastering house walls with manure, husking grain, sorting onions, and picking stones out of lentils. Finally, when they are involved directly in selling commercial crops, it is usually in the sale of small amounts of vegetables, left over from household consumption, on a seasonal basis at the nearby market in Saswad. In all these cases, the amounts of money that pass through female hands rarely exceed 100 rupees at a time. (In 1981–82 the US$ fluctuated between 9 and 10 rupees on the foreign exchange market.) This upper ceiling is set by average remittances from working husbands in cities. The lower limit, which represents the far more frequently handled sums, is in the range of the 4 to 8 rupees a day that women make for agricultural labor, depending on the season and the task. In between these parameters are the proceeds of low-level local sale of vegetables. Not only do women deal with small sums of money gained and spent in a series of small dealings (to be described below), they are, by extension, involved in allocative moves over smaller periods, though they are frequently aware of issues that span weeks, months, even years. That is, women may, and do, have in the back of their minds problems of grain shortages, sharecropping contracts, forthcoming marriages, and ritual commitments that may place the horizons of their attention over an extended temporal landscape. But the bulk of their energy is necessarily devoted to matters that recur in a shorter time frame. This is nowhere truer than in the domain of food, which I shall come to shortly.

Further, the social universe in which women are embedded on a daily basis is on the whole restricted to a small number of persons and to a space that is closely tied to their houses and neighborhoods, by comparison to the numerical and spatial scope of the social worlds of adult men. This is not, of course, to deny that women often deal with strangers, that they often go long distances to work in someone else's fields or their own, that they sometimes maintain links with kinsmen and affines in villages far away, or that they occasionally conduct religiously inspired journeys to places outside the district. All this is true, yet, when compared with men (as we shall see in the next section on the sociality of subsistence), women's dealings take place in a numerically and spatially more confined world.

Closely linked to the small scale of the interactional world of women is its intricacy.[5] This is a somewhat subtler point that is closer to the central thrust of this chapter. Women deal not only with fewer people, over smaller units of time, with smaller amounts of cash or kind, but their dealings are more intricate when compared with those of men. That is, over any given short period, such as a few hours, a day, or even a week, women are likely to be shifting their attention very rapidly, and they are likely to be engaged in attending to several tasks at once. This means that their attention has to be more intricately and more involutedly allocated between foreground and background issues.

---

5.   The use of the term "intricacy" here is intended to characterize the experiential aspect or aspects of women's work in many societies, whose behavioral complexity has frequently been noted. It also overlaps to some degree with the use of the terms "intricacy" and "complexity" in Douglas and Gross (1981) and in Douglas (1984). However, Mary Douglas's emphasis is on the macrointricacy of rule systems, whereas my emphasis is on the microintricacy of attention and action, from the actor's perspective.

This intricacy is not only a function of the small scale and high turnover of many of the things they are handling but also arises because the handling of these various tasks is not spatially segregated, as it often is with men's work. Thus, women at market are often minding children at the same time; when they go out to gather firewood, they might need to attend to their goats (and possibly their children) simultaneously. Sometimes all these tasks are constrained by the objective of getting food to husbands or sons in the fields. Frequently, such a heavily overlaid and intricate schedule is further complicated by critical tasks (such as being at someone else's house or fields for work) that cannot easily be manipulated. Intricacy has another, more literal dimension as well. Women are frequently involved in mending clothes, fixing small tools, making minor repairs to the house, tending chronic ailments of animals, constructing temporary ritual designs of chalk inside or outside the home, and other activities that require focusing intensely on microdesigns, whether physical, aesthetic, or structural. Examples of the intricacy of women's dealings can be multiplied, and more will be said about this quality in relation to food at the end of this section and in relation to sociality in the next.

The frequency of women's engagements adds the final twist to the picture of small-scale, intricate actions. They must shift from locus to locus (from field to house to stream to market to temple to someone else's threshing ground); from transaction to transaction (from the village shop to the doctor to a sharecropping partner to a sick friend); from social frame to social frame (from dyadic nurture of an infant to friendly rebuke of a daughter to an ongoing quarrel with a neighbor to an ambiguous relationship with a friend to a humiliating encounter with a creditor to an abusive relationship with an employer); and from medium to medium (from dealings in food to dealings in cash to dealings in pots and pans to dealings in animal manure). Such shifts, and many others like them, mean that the transactional world of women in Vadi is not only composed of small-scale dealings, of intricate and interweaving demands for attention and action, but also that the small scale and intricacy of transactions are compounded by the high frequency of shifts, in the venue, frame, and medium, of these transactions. Together, these changes add up to a world that is, in regard to the conscious attention of women, miniaturized, fluid, and fast moving.

Let us now use one extended example to look more closely at the implications of these qualities for the domestic handling of foods. It is based on my interaction on a day in April 1982 with a woman called

S., who lives with her husband in Vadi. She is somewhat better off than many women in the village. She and her husband still control their small plots of land and are therefore able to assert authority over both their sons (one is unmarried and lives with them, while the other lives nearby with his wife).

"I am very weary today," S. begins. "Therefore I did not cook at all. In a little while I am going to make a little spiced rice [*fodnicha bhat*]." She then says she is going to get some cooked vegetable (*bhaji*) from her daughter-in-law, who lives nearby. Coming back with some lentil soup and sorghum bread, she continues: "Yesterday was an important ritual day, and someone from every house had to make the journey to Shikhat Singhnapur [a nearby pilgrimage site]. They all had to be given *bhaji puri*" [a bread and vegetable combination] and *puran poli* [a special sweet bread] for this journey."

At this juncture her husband shows up and says he is off to the pilgrimage site. He asks S. whether she has any *bhakri* (bread, here loosely meaning "food"); she says she does not but will go and see if someone else has any. Meanwhile, her husband goes off to try to collect some money owed to him by another man.

S. then states that she has only one small plot (*vavar*), from which she just got a harvest of onions and sold it for Rs. 900. She intends, she says, to dole this money out to her sons. She gave Rs. 250 to one of them yesterday, who, instead of buying grain, bought a cot. She was so furious that he went back and got one bag of grain. "Now the remaining money has to be given to people in Saswad [the nearby market town]. I had to leave my nose-ring with a doctor who is giving me injections and pills for my health, and I have to give him some money and reclaim it." Her husband then returns with Rs. 10. S. gets angry with him and asks how he dare come back with this paltry sum. She takes out a Rs. 100 note, and he gives her Rs. 70 back. She then gives him two pieces of bread for his trip.

This vignette is unusual in some respects, for S. clearly has more authority in her household than many women in Vadi do, though they are not generally reticent about expressing their views. Also, the relatively large sums of money that are being handled here reflect the fact that harvests of commercial vegetables occur in April. But so do the demands of debtors, of ritual, and of less-than-provident males like S.'s son, who indulges his desire for a Western-style cot over a stock of grain. But most of all, this episode illustrates the small flows of food between households that are going on all the time in Vadi and the very complex transactional frames within which they occur. Finally, this vignette illustrates very nicely the intercalibration of ritual, market, and debt periodicities that frames dietary decisions at the household level. Also, though S. is different from many women in not having small children to feed, she does illustrate the flexibility of daily food production in the house and the weariness (*kantala*) that sometimes pushes women to simplify their own cooking and draw on kin and neighbors for short-term food needs. The social prerequisites of such flexibility are dealt with in the next section. Finally, for reasons that were not entirely clear to me, S. told her husband that she had no food to give him, though she had just gotten some from her daughter-in-law, part of which she did subsequently give him. This was clearly a small move in some ongoing micropolitical dealings in food in this extended family (Appadurai 1981).

Small-scale food flows are not only to be seen in the amicable borrowing of cooked food. (The term for such borrowing is *usne*, which means any friendly loan that does not entail interest: it can involve food, money, tools, or virtually anything else.) It also goes on between households in the matter of vegetables, grain, tea, sugar, and milk. But small-scale food transactions are mainly seen in the village grocery shops, where women come in all the time to buy oil, grain, lentils, spices, tea, or sugar in amounts (often a handful) that seem unbelievably small to the outsider's eye and that are doubtless economically inefficient purchases. But given the small-denomination, high-velocity circulation of money through female hands, there is frequently no alternative to such transactions.

At the same time, women are continuously monitoring (though here it is very difficult to generalize about the degree of conscious attention with which they do this) the quantity and nature of what is coming off their own plots, the market prices and availabilities of what is not in their own harvests, and the current or prospective arrival of visitors and guests, especially in the postharvest festival season. In doing this, they rely on their experience from past years about how long their basic grain stocks might last (the critical question) and how long stocks of other staples (if such stocks exist) can be expected to last. Finally, in making daily dietary decisions, the flow of money from any sort of income, as well as the degree of pressure to pay off what seem to be never-ending debts, has to be constantly assessed, as do the choices of what to cook, how to cook it, how much to cook, and when to cook it.

It is in the context of this sort of small-scale, fluid, and microscopic manipulation of food flows and claims that women are constantly adjusting the modular, stratified, and seasonal structure of the dietary inventory that I discussed in the preceding section. At all times, the pressures of sociality (whatever they may be) have to be weighed against the contingencies of the domestic economy itself. In this conjuncture, all women have a clear idea of what they might like to cook from meal to meal, from day to day, and from season to season. But what they actually cook is the continuously shifting (and indirect) product of the interweaving of other pressures through the hearth. Both the sources of, and the solutions to, some of these dilemmas lie outside the household in transdomestic forms of sociality, and it is to the discussion of these forms that I now turn.

The Sociality of Subsistence

Studies of domestic dietary decisions too often convey the impression that domestic food decisions occur in functional and psychological isolation from the larger world of production and community life. From the vantage point of women in Vadi, a variety of social processes penetrates the hearth constantly. But equally, the requirements of food provision press men and women into particular ways of being social.

I have already mentioned that small-scale loans of food are an important aspect of life in Vadi. These movements of food between households are part of a very complex world of social relations, principally between women. In the first place, they reflect the widespread recognition by women that without such small flows (reciprocal at least in theory and over the long run) most households would find themselves occasionally in distress. For the kinds of periodicities and contingencies discussed throughout this chapter imply that there will frequently be needs for such loans.

But the fact is that such needs themselves arise because of the larger social worlds within which the households of Vadi are embedded. When the out-migrant man or men of the household come to visit Vadi, both the pace of social life and commensal complexity increase. Other men are likely to visit, and the resident male will probably extend invitations to them to stay and have a meal, frequently without any advance notice. Such contingencies can be fairly common for those women whose husbands work in Pune (which is only about twenty-five miles away), as frequent as once every week or two. In the case of men who work in Mumbai, the visits are likely to be lengthier but less frequent, and they usually coincide with peak periods of agricultural or ritual activity, most often in April, May, and June. Sometimes, these periods coincide with increases in cash flow, since the absent men like to show their largess when they visit, however incapable they are of sending regular remittances during the rest of the year. At the very least, such unexpected entertainment of guests means that tea (with milk and sugar if at all possible) must be offered.

It is in these circumstances that, if a household has run out of its own sugar, someone (usually a young son or daughter) must run to the store for a small-scale transaction. If the woman of the house does not have her own goat, she needs to have one or more relationships with women who do so that she can get small amounts of milk at short notice. Such small-scale transactions in milk, sugar, and sometimes tea leaves are the most frequent and humble of these interhousehold movements of food. Maintaining good relations with friends, kinsmen, or affines, especially in one's immediate neighborhood, is critical if one is to have access to these forms of credit. One way to assure such access is, of course, to be responsive to such needs on the part of others whenever possible. This form of pressure to maintain social relations in one's neighborhood is, of course, magnified when one wishes to borrow more substantial items, such as grain, vegetables, oil, or lentils.

Another avenue through which the larger world of Vadi is articulated with household dietary flows and contingencies is the ritual process. Vadi is a thoroughly Hindu village, and its Hinduism is deeply embedded in the geography and religious history of Maharashtra, particularly in the songs of the poet-saints of the medieval period and the shrines of the regional incarnations of the great gods of Hinduism. Village families make pilgrimages to a variety of sacred places, some of which (like Alandi, Jejuri, and Pandharpur) are more cosmopolitan in their reach and others of which are more narrow in their significance, such as the temples of Kalubai and Khandoba. In the course of the year, there are smaller, village-based observances dedicated to a variety of deities, some calendric and some timed by individual households. In addition, there are important days during which ancestor shrines (*pitr*) in the fields are given food offerings or lineage deities in the village are worshipped. There are six shrines in the village, but the one at which the most important collective celebrations (including the major village festival of the year, simply referred to as *urus*) take place is the Vitthala temple.

In addition to these celebrations, which are inspired by the particular stories and theories associated with specific deities, there are a large variety of life-cycle rituals, the most important of which are the massive feasts associated with birth and death. The common element in these ritual events—whether they are collective or domestic, calendric or life-cycle, large-scale or small-scale, oriented to fertility or to prosperity—is the place of special foods in them. The gods and the ancestors, depending upon the context, demand special foods, the most important of which is *puran poli* (a wholewheat pan-fried bread with a jaggery and clarified butter filling), the quintessential festive food. At such large-scale social events as marriage and death ceremonies, the meals tend to be maximal elaborations of normal domestic fare. Especially at the height of the marriage and festival season, but to some extent throughout the year, women are frequently engaged in preparing one or another kind of festive food, either for themselves and their immediate coresidents, as contributions for collective offerings to various deities, or for taking along for subsistence and for offering on pilgrimages. Marriages (which cluster together after the winter harvest in the hot months of April and May) and deaths occasion large-scale feasts (involving from a hundred to a thousand guests). At such times, the domestic economies of the host household (and, to some extent, the host lineage) are completely subordinated to the exigencies of public commensality. Such events leave their mark, through mechanisms of financial and social debt, during the months and even the years to come.

The point of the relationship between this complex and differentiated ritual process and the domestic dietary process is that it is multidimensional. It involves an ongoing set of demands for special, high-cost, labor-intensive foods, and sometimes for large amounts of them. But these demands cut both ways. On the one hand, they represent an additional source of stress for women who are already dealing with a large number of exigencies. On the other hand, they represent a deeply meaningful form of give and take, that provides, in the Hindu world, the stuff of social relations at levels ranging from the family to the village and beyond. In addition, insofar as these special foods are directed to deities, ancestors, and spirits who dwell in houses, in village temples, in fields, in wells, in streams, and in larger regional shrines, they are part of the great Hindu cycle of dealings with divinity, whose reward is the productivity of the land, the fertility of women, and the prosperity of the household.

In thus responding to the exigencies of the ritual calendar, women in particular are simultaneously interacting on three levels with the world around them: with the world as a source of demands and limits, both logistical and social; with the world as a place of persons (deities, kinsmen, friends, guests, and even strangers), who require special treatment but who are one's own source of security in ways that are direct and indirect, short- and long-term, specific and diffuse; and, finally, with the world as a scheme of divine persons and forces that return, transvalued, the sustenance given to them, both as *prasad* (sacred food) and as prosperity. From the practical point of view, ritual and festive food, its preparation, its exchange, and its consumption, constitutes the moral center of the habitus of the villagers of Vadi. For it is in the context of ritual food that the harsh reality of economizing (*katkasar karne*) in an agricultural milieu is repeatedly transformed into the experience of meaningful sociality and moral renewal. This sort of ritual-inspired food preparation best captures the double edge of all women's work in a peasant society such as Vadi: toilsome and distracting on the one hand, but pivotal to the reproduction of the group as a moral entity on the other.

Women recognize this complex relationship of food to social and moral renewal in the inverse of feasting, fasting (*upavas*). Fasting is a very important aspect of practical religion in Hindu India, and so it is in Vadi. Most households have at least one member who fasts at least one day a week, and if it is just one person who fasts it is likely to be the senior woman. However, men and boys also fast, usually in association with their voluntary devotion to a specific deity. For adult women, such regularized fasting is also usually connected to a vow (*navas*) to some particular (usually regional) deity related to some specific boon, either granted or prayed for. Fasting involves, as elsewhere in India, renouncing grains—not all food—and relying on other foods. In Vadi, as elsewhere in Maharashtra, the standard "fasting food" is tapioca (*sabudana*) made into a sort of stew (*khichdi*), sometimes supplemented by fruit. Even fasting can be an occasion for sociality, since friends or kinswomen sometimes bring each other these foods on fast ending days. Thus even the fasting periodicities of women who live or work in proximity can affect each other significantly.

Finally, the small- and large-scale provision of food to households other than one's own, sometimes in small and spontaneous ways and at other times in predictable and more substantial forms, is tied to subsistence through another kind of sociality, the informal female work group. The term for such work groups (whether of men or of women) is *varangula*. When men use this word it refers to a precisely structured, enduring agreement involving at least two and usually no more than four men, to pool bullocks and tools for specific agricultural activities, mainly involving the beginning of the farming year. Women's *varangula* groups, however, are larger because the tasks in which they are involved (like onion planting or harvesting) demand more workers. They are also more variable and fluid in their composition and are more closely tied to friendships and kinship relationships that are fortified by spatial proximity. Information about the need for such work groups, the likelihood of being asked to participate in them, and the ability to draw on smaller, informal versions of them to do minor household tasks depends on keeping these networks lubricated through the reciprocities of food.

Friendships in this female world are very complex, conflicted, and pivotal. For women must maintain relations with other women (whether kinswomen or neighbors) who constitute their more or less permanent local support groups; the monitors of their own domestic lives; the potential sources of nasty gossip, but also of critical support when it is needed; and the keys to vital information and opportunities for participation in remunerative work groups. Maintaining these networks, often in the face of other pressing demands on one's resources, is the other modality through which production and consumption are socially interdigitated. For one's friendships with one's female neighbors, like the demands of gods, guests, and husbands, entail expenditures of time and energy that women experience as exhausting. Yet, as sources of compassion, loans, moral support at critical moments, protection from irate husbands, information about work, and just as shoulders to cry on, these friendships are the mainstay of adult female life in Vadi. But keeping up these friendships also requires a willingness to make small loans of food, to share food freely when one is in the fields with a work group, and to give a share of cooked food to lineage, neighborhood, or village festivities.

In all these ways, the dietary decisions of the hearth are deeply connected to the worlds of the neighborhood, the fields, the marketplace, and even to the religious life of the region. Each of these other arenas implies a different form and kind of sociality, and each one is Janus-faced, representing harsh budgetary exigencies on one side and moral security and social standing on the other. This is the dual link between sociality and subsistence in the lived experience of the women of Vadi.

Conclusion: Exigency and Improvisation in Dietary Strategy

I have sought to capture the texture of domestic dietary strategies, as I construe it, in the lives of some women in Vadi. Two analytic points have been made in the course of this descriptive account. The first is that women's transactions are small-scale, intricate, and frequent. The second is that if we trace the paths of women's attention we are inevitably forced to see that dietary decisions are intimately connected to problems that have to do with other larger and more public arenas of social life. It remains now to ask what the implications of these two points are for an adequate characterization of the quality of dietary strategies at the domestic level.

Schutz (1970) whom I cite in the first paragraph of this chapter, makes a distinction, in his account of how human beings render some parts of their environment more relevant than others, between "theme" and "horizon" (Schutz 1970). The former is an element that is in the foreground of the attention of the actor and is subject to conscious scrutiny and manipulation. The horizon consists of whatever sets the backdrop, the frame, the boundaries of the actor's ongoing (and ever-shifting) mental landscape. Looked at from this perspective, the first conclusion to be drawn from my description is that dietary decisions are rarely explicit, systematic, conscious, or set apart from other issues in the way that many analyses imply. Using Schutz's terms, and following the description I have constructed, it should be noted that the relationship between "horizon" and "theme," between background and foreground issues, is continuously shifting for the women of Vadi. On the whole, and except when there is a truly unusual configuration of circumstances, daily dietary choice is made in what Gladwin and Murtaugh (1980) would call a "pre-attentive manner," and dietary issues remain in the background of women's attention. In this regard, dietary decisions are no more privileged than the other activities in which women must engage, and they move into the foreground of women's attention only insofar as, and for so long as, they present a more pressing or more puzzling choice than some other one.

This is not a peculiar artifact of mental structure in Vadi. It is a function of the sorts of issues, far transcending the hearth and the meal, in which dietary strategies are embedded. At the same time, women can carry on the task of providing food to the members of their household in a largely pre-attentive manner because an important part of their habitus is a mental inventory, a stance, and a disposition that allow them to deploy their shifting assets effectively. Such strategizing is neither a mechanical following of "rules" nor an ad hoc and culture-free response to exigency. It is an example of what Bourdieu has called "regulated improvisation," a characteristic of important aspects of social life in many stable societies. But it seems especially true of peasant societies, more still of their domestic settings, and is nowhere better exemplified than in the daily strategies of women for feeding their families.

Acknowledgments

This chapter was written while the author was a Fellow at the Center for Advanced Study in the Behavioral Sciences at Stanford University in California. Financial support during this period was provided by the National Science Foundation (BNS 8011494) and by the University of Pennsylvania. Fieldwork in Maharashtra, India, during 1981 and 1982 was supported by the National Science Foundation, the American Institute for Indian Studies, and the Social Science Research Council. Carol Breckenridge provided useful comments and criticisms on an earlier draft of this chapter, as did the editors of the original volume.

CHAPTER 5

Technology and the Reproduction of Values in Rural Western India

Introduction: Morality, Politics, and Technological Change

The problem of assessing the costs of economic change in any society is simultaneously moral and political. It is moral because it involves problems of autonomy and coercion, and because it involves cross-cultural and intrasocial debates about value. It is political because it entails decisions about *whose* preferences count, *what* criteria to use in assessing such preferences, and *how* to establish acceptable grounds for a genuine debate about development.

The body of this chapter is devoted to the presentation of a highly specific setting—a village in Western India—and a highly specific technological change—the electrification of traditional open-surface wells. But embedded in these specifics are a host of larger processes and more general issues. Though my argument depends, in part, on my interpretation of the commercialization of agriculture in Maharashtra in the last century, its general assumptions are anticipated in this introduction.

Any moral and political assessment of technological change encounters the following major dilemma: is there any reasonable middle ground, in assessing the pros and cons of technological change, between using some variety of Euro-American utilitarianism and succumbing to some radical form of relativist cultural protectionism? My own approach to this dilemma is as follows. I am firmly opposed to *any* technical calculus of welfare which operates on criteria that are wholly external to the moral and cultural values of the community whose future is at stake. This position rests on the notion that imposed change (and, by extension, imposed criteria for the assessment of change) is on a priori grounds unacceptable because it is, in the most general sense, anti-democratic. But in a world in which at least some members of rural communities appear to desire and seize the opportunities offered by new technologies, how shall we assess the worth of technological change?

One class of answers to this question is fundamentally distributional in its orientation and takes as a key consideration the matter of how widely and deeply the gains of technological change are distributed. The trouble with this solution is that it is a version of the utilitarian solution, and contains no provisions for taking into account the moral and cultural fabric of the community as a value in its own right (in my terms, as a prime value). Instead it relies on some explicit or implicit aggregation of preferences, whose ultimate ground is *individual* choices, preferences, and benefits. I shall return to the problem of individualism shortly.

I am also opposed to what I have called the position of radical cultural protectionism, which would suggest that the preservation of any coherent cultural system is a prime value, which requires no further justification. Here I have two objections. The first is that this argument relies on an implicit valuation of cultural difference as an end in itself. This valuation comes out of a relatively recent Euro-American orientation, which is often used to enslave other communities in invented ideas about their own authenticity. That is, one product of the encounter between the West and the non-Western world in the post-Renaissance period has been a series of anthropological and protoanthropological efforts to create ideas about "authentic natives," as opposed to those who are somehow believed to have been corrupted by contact with the outside world. This generally invidious contrast frequently forms the basis for discussing the relative authenticity of other cultures on the basis of criteria in the control of the Western observer. Authenticity is, in any case, a Western concern with a relatively short history.

Second, this argument can be (and is) often used to justify a variety of inhumane and undesirable cultural practices, along with whatever is valuable within a given cultural system. What Lévi-Strauss once said about functionalism ([1963] 1967: 13) can usefully be pirated in the following form: to say that any culture is valuable is a truism, but to say that everything in a culture is valuable is an absurdity. How then are we to assess change from a moral point of view?

One step towards an answer involves the relationship between relatively narrow, "economistic" criteria for assessing technological change and broader, more "holistic" ones, centered on the reproduction of the core cultural values of a community. Although the distinction between these two sorts of criteria is analytically fairly clear, there are situations where the two criteria not only lead to similar assessments, *but must necessarily do so*. This convergence of assessments is likely to occur when technological change is accompanied by losses of indigenous knowledge. My empirical case represents just such a situation.

To identify the conditions for such convergence, it is necessary to specify the critical differences between "economistic" and "holistic" criteria for the assessment of technological change. Let us note the important similarities between these two kinds of criteria: both are value orientations towards technical change; both claim to be oriented, in the last analysis, to collective well-being; and both are grounded in some sort of moral universalism. The crucial difference, however, lies in the relative importance of the individual in each of them. In all varieties (however broadly based) of economistic assessment, the individual is seen both as the crucial locus of agency and as the prime moral value. In more holistic frameworks, the prime value is the reproduction of communities and the important loci of agency are usually various kinds of groups and collectivities. The emergence of individualism as a moral orientation in European thought (and its cross-cultural implications) constitutes a very large subject which can hardly be fully engaged here. For one thing, the links (and distinctions) between ideas about the self (which have a long history), the rise of the individual, the formation of a commercial ethos, and the rise of a market culture, even in the West, have hardly been fully worked out.

The situation is murkier still when we look at this matter from a comparative perspective. While we have good grounds to believe that the relatively recent Euro-American valuation of the individual runs against the moral grain of many other societies, we can hardly deny that in many of these other societies complex commercial cultures have existed (even prior to Western contact), as have complex, gain-oriented, patterns of calculation. Sorting out this labyrinth of issues, which involves carefully distinguishing between different ideas about the self or person, different formats for the cultural organization of commerce, different modalities for calculation, and different patterns of market orientation, is an important task which is still very much in its infancy. For my purposes, I shall be concerned with the *sort* of individualism that arose in the Western

Indian experience of commercialization in the last century. This does not preclude the possibility that other forms of individualism may have preexisted in Western India or risen in the last century; nor does it deny the fact that in Western India, and elsewhere in the world, there were very important links between markets and the countryside long before this past century. My concern here is with one such articulation of the "individual" and one such experience of commercialization.

Since my axiomatic starting point is the *value of reproduction* (as an entitlement of all human communities), it is important to specify what exactly the reproduction of a community entails. It entails the reproduction of its central social forms, as expressions of its core values. This commitment to the value of reproduction does not contradict my earlier statement of opposition to radical cultural protectionism, since the latter is usually built around values and principles imposed on the community by some external agency, usually with some exogenous perspective, while the former is based (at least in principle) on an effort to discover endogenous criteria for the reproduction of community. Nevertheless, in practice, there is a danger that the more desirable of these two positions (from my perspective) might lead one into the less desirable one. But that is a risk that must be run.

In the case of the rural community in Western India which constitutes my main source of data, the core values, and thus the central social forms, revolve around *sociality* itself. This is not simply yet another instance of Durkheim's general theory about the primacy of society over the individual, which probably holds for all societies, and whose genealogy goes back to Aristotle. Rather, I intend to suggest that in this community (and others of its type) much of what is seen as valuable by members of the community, and much of what appears to underlie the central traditional forms of social life, are linkages between persons and groups, taken for granted not only as means but also as ends. If it can be shown, in such a situation, that the *prime value of sociality* is eroded by a particular process of technological change, we have grounds to regard the change in question as inimical to the reproduction of the community.

The convergence between this ("holistic") reason for criticizing technological change, and any one of a number of narrower, more "economistic" reasons for criticism, lies in the relationship between knowledge and technological change. In many traditional agrarian societies (and probably in some nonagrarian ones as well) it is difficult to distinguish technical knowledge very clearly from knowledge which is tied to larger normative and social ends. In such societies, *techne* and *episteme* (to borrow

Stephen Marglin's use of the Greek terms)[1] are both embedded in wider social, religious, and epistemological grounds and contexts. In turn, this leads me to suggest that the question of the "decoupling" of various technologies from their primary cultural settings and entailments to new cultural settings may best be attacked, in the first instance, at the level of knowledge, rather than at the level of practice or organization.

From this perspective, the critical fact about the commercialization of agriculture in Western India in the last century is that it creates a new distinction between technical knowledge and its larger epistemological context. The emergence of an *agronomic episteme*, divorced from a wider *agrarian* discourse, represents just such a separation of knowledge from context, in the process of which the corresponding techne is rendered obsolete. In this process, the very epistemological fabric of the community is also rendered obsolescent and survives only in the diminished form.

This is the epistemological precursor of the corrosion of the prime value of sociality. It is in such situations, where technological change creates a (previously meaningless) distinction between technical knowledge and broader modes of knowing, that utilitarian criteria for assessing such change lead to the same conclusions as broader criteria involving cultural reproduction. For change of this sort tends simultaneously to involve a reduction of options (and an increase of risks) for individuals and groups, and lead to a corrosion of core cultural values. It is this sort of double jeopardy which I will seek to illustrate in my account of the process of commercialization of agriculture in Western India.

Agriculture in Maharashtra

The state of Maharashtra in Western India was formed in 1960, after the Bombay Presidency of British India was split into the linguistic states of Maharashtra and Gujarat. But Maharashtra, as a linguistic, religious, and cultural region, has an identity going back at least eight hundred years which undergirds current conceptions of the cultural unity of the state. Maharashtra is an interesting state because it combines a relatively advanced industrial sector (producing fertilizers, heavy machinery, drugs, textiles, and motorized transport) and a sophisticated financial

---

1.   Marglin used these terms in the introduction to the volume in which this chapter was originally published, Marglin and Marglin 1990.

and commercial sector, centered on the city of Mumbai, with a relatively impoverished agricultural sector.

The agricultural sector in Maharashtra has a profile which is deeply rooted in its ecological and historical circumstances. The state can be roughly divided into a narrow coastal strip, which is very densely populated, has a very high rainfall, and is massively involved in rice production, and a very large plateau (part of the Deccan Plateau) on the other side of the hill range known as the Western Ghats, which is characterized by low rainfall, low population densities, and a production profile dominated by millets (sorghum and pearl millet) and pulses. This very gross ecological contrast, of course, conceals finer distinctions, particularly in the plateau region, where there are differences in the degree of urbanization, the number and accessibility of market centers, the quality of soil, and the amount of rainfall. In keeping with these, and other, differences, the history and nature of penetration of rural communities by the forces of commercialization is also varied.

The village in which I worked (described in detail in a subsequent section) is located at the western edge of this dry agrarian region, near the city of Pune, and is only six hours (by bus and train) from Mumbai. It is part of Pune district, which in terms of the intensity of irrigation, the amount of land devoted to commercial crops, the numbers of males who work in cities (while their families remain in the villages), etc., represents a more diverse profile than many of the other dry districts. Pune district, though it contains subregions which are rain-deficient and largely devoted to subsistence cereal cropping, also has many pockets of intensely commercialized agriculture. In particular, this district is responsible for a large share of the sugarcane production of Maharashtra state, which is in turn a very significant proportion of the sugarcane production of all of India. It also has a very important share in the production of vegetables and pulses for regional markets, as also of wheat and rice production in the state. Pune district thus represents a complex agrarian profile, with a fairly substantial history of commercialized agriculture. As we shall see, the village I studied reflects this history in important ways.

The intensity of commercial agriculture in Maharashtra, as in many other rain-deficient parts of South Asia, is critically determined by access to man-made irrigation techniques, principal among which are canals and wells. It is my impression that the relative importance of wells to commercial agriculture is greater in Maharashtra than in any other Indian state. But wells, as we shall see, are a very complex and intricate part of the total agrarian world of rural Maharashtra. Changes in their technology have a historical context which transcends the technological dimension, and which involves the emergence of an agronomic discourse in Western India in the last century.

Commercialization and Agricultural Discourse

It is notoriously difficult to get reliable historical information at the village level, especially regarding the sorts of epistemological and moral shifts that accompany technical change in a domain such as agriculture. The bulk of the historical sources are colonial records and reports which have a particular epistemological and rhetorical structure (Saumerez Smith 1985), one that does not encourage the sort of cultural analysis in which I am engaged. But there is a type of document which can be used to chart, at least in a very rough way, shifts in indigenous ideology which instantiate the conceptual costs of technical change. In the Maharashtrian case, I have been fortunate to discover certain nineteenth-century tracts concerning agriculture which provide a benchmark against which I can compare current "official" discourse concerning agriculture contained in such sources as farmer's magazines, diaries produced for farmers, texts produced by and for agricultural universities, and so on. What a sampling of these texts (all of which are in Marathi) permits is some rough approximation of the contours of epistemological change in agricultural thought in Maharashtra.[2]

It is important to understand that these sources constitute varieties of "official" ideology and they do not by any means bring us the direct voice of the farmer, particularly the small farmer. Indeed, they all constitute efforts to persuade farmers in Maharashtra to undertake new kinds of agricultural practices. They are thus rhetorical in structure, and reflect the forces of commercialization as they linguistically and conceptually impinge upon farmers. It is difficult to know exactly how many farmers read (or had indirect access to) such texts—either in the past or in the present—and it is therefore hazardous to infer much about their effects on farmers. What they do permit is a picture of the changing assumptions of official agricultural ideologies, and of the way in which an indigenous agronomy is formed that reshapes, selects, and eliminates

---

2.   The Marathi texts I have used are all to be found in the India Office Library (London) and are the following: Amruttungal 1852; Apte 1890; K. Khare 1882; and Nipunge 1981.

important parts of village-level agricultural knowledge. The analysis of these changing assumptions permits a rough corroboration of the case for cultural change that I have made in the subsequent parts of this paper, and a more precise linguistic sense of how commercialization is made a locally credible and inexorable process.

The benchmark text that I have used, Amruttungal (1852), is in the form of a dialogue between a learned and widely traveled Brahman and a Kunbi farmer in the town of Paithan in Aurangabad district, one of the driest and still least modernized parts of rural Maharashtra. Without providing much justification for its main assumption, the text takes for granted that this cosmopolitan Brahman has much to teach the Kunbi farmer and his four sons, who are portrayed as struggling to eke out a subsistence existence on their holdings. The text constitutes a fascinating glimpse of what, in the middle of the nineteenth century, was seen by some Maharashtrians as the cutting edge of rural commercialization.

The most striking thing about this text is that it confirms the extent to which an extensive commercial vocabulary was already in use in the agricultural sector. The lexicon of commercialization in this text is centered around costs (*kharcha*) and their reduction, increases in yield (*utpanna*), the frequent use of the concepts of profit (*nafā*) and loss (*thōtā*), and the idea of the commodity (*jinnas*). Together, these terms are used in sentences attributed both to the "expert" Brahman and to the Kunbi peasants, in ways that express the central rhetorical goal of this text—increased agricultural yield and income. The main chapters are devoted to advertising the commercial virtues and the principal techniques associated with growing new varieties of local cultigens (like sugarcane); new cultigens from Europe like potatoes and fodder grass; and the value of breeding animals like goats and horses.

What is interesting about this rhetoric of new agricultural opportunities and techniques (firmly couched in the commercial idiom discussed above) is that it does not yet use the concept of the "progressive" or "modern" (*ādhūnik*) farmer, but speaks only of the clever or competent (*hushār*) farmer. Further, the agricultural message is couched in terms of a generalized preaching of the virtues of the European regime: separate chapters are devoted to the importance of literacy and the virtues of Christianity (the book was apparently written by a local convert); and there is a fascinating chapter which tries to allay the fears of the farmer regarding the newly introduced coinage of the East India Company, by preaching the associated virtues of standardization, free exchange, elimination of middlemen, and so on. Thus we can see that, at least at this stage, the commercialization of agriculture is seen as part of a general "rationalization" of rural life, in the domains of education, religion, and commerce.

Yet, when we look closely at the language of commercialization and its accompanying epistemological framework, it is quite different from later "official tracts." For one thing, the concept of capital (*bhāṇndval*) is not used once in the entire text. Though it was probably in use in other commercial contexts in mid-nineteenth-century Maharashtra, it does not appear to have been a critical requirement of the rhetoric of commercializing interests in agriculture. Thus, unlike later texts, in which it is noted that certain improvements pose major challenges in terms of "capital," in this early text the matter is simply seen as one of "costs" and associated gains. By extension, agriculture as a whole is not yet seen as a commercial enterprise, in which investment, saving, and capitalization are seen as the critical engines of profit. Rather, profit is seen in proto-capitalistic accounting terms, as a matter of reducing costs and seizing opportunities to make bigger profits largely by increasing yields and by exploiting new cultigens and animals.

Finally, it is interesting to note that a series of things which are problematic for small farmers are here simply taken for granted as unproblematic features of the agrarian landscape. Thus, though the section on sugarcane makes much of its need for water, wells and their management are simply not mentioned, nor is the problem of water more generally. Land is also treated tacitly as an expanding resource. Finally, though there are brief mentions of problems of labor, on the whole there is a model of family farming in which the problems of hired labor are yet to emerge. Lastly, credit for agricultural investments is not treated as a major problem in the economics of farming. It does appear in the section on currency, where it is seen as part of the evil stranglehold of moneylenders and absentee landlords. Credit is thus still part of the social universe of dependency and debt, rather than a part of the progressive framework of investment and enterprise.

In general, the picture we get from this 1852 text is one of an incipiently commercialized but not an aggressively entrepreneurial agricultural world, which is just being exposed to new cultigens as well as new forms of currency, religion, and literacy. Though it is a discourse which is underpinned by the language of profit and loss, there are only the beginnings of a thoroughgoing ethos of economizing, and it portrays small farmers as averse to risks, subsistence-oriented, and suspicious of new agricultural and commercial techniques and instruments.

The situation is much changed by the latter part of the nineteenth century. The two texts which I have consulted, Khare (1882) and Apte (1890), show a vastly more complicated view of the agrarian process and its commercial dimensions. This is no surprise, given that by 1880, with the impact of the railways and the linkage of many parts of rural Maharashtra to regional and world markets in sugarcane, cotton, rice, and wheat, great changes were underway. Population growth, the extension of agriculture, the pursuit of commercial opportunities—all of which characterize the period from 1870 to 1920—had already transformed the rural landscape in important ways.[3]

The first of these texts, Khare (1882), is at once a polemic about the sad plight of the Maharashtrian farmer and his exploitation by urban people, moneylenders, and the state, and a manual for progressive farming techniques and objectives. It thus anticipates the anti-urban, activist ethos of the powerful farmers' movements in Maharashtra in the later 1970s and early 1980s. In its critique of external commercial interests, particularly those of *baniyas* (businessmen) and others from the North, it provides a rich glimpse of the ideological ethos of the Deccan riots of 1875.

Although it is ostensibly a powerful plea on behalf of hard-pressed farmers, its central assumption is the ignorance of farmers whose lack of knowledge (*gyān*) is seen as the principal reason for their poverty. This sense that farmers do not know what they need to know (already implicit in the 1852 tract) is now explicit, and it expresses the formal announcement of the gap between "official" agronomic knowledge and the traditional knowledge of farmers in this region. More generally, by this period we witness the formation of an indigenous agronomic discourse in which the knowledge of farmers is simply absorbed into a larger, more rationalized discourse, framed in information and exhortation concerning new techniques and goals. That is, a large part of these new tracts

---

3. My general sense of the social, political, and economic transformation of agriculture in South Asia in the last century has been especially informed by the following four collections of essays: Bayliss-Smith and Wanmali 1984; Chaudhari and Dewey 1979; Desai, Rudolph, and Rudra 1984; and D. Kumar and Desai 1983. As far as the agrarian transformation of Maharashtra is concerned, I have benefited greatly from the following: Attwood 1980, 1984; Banaji 1977; Catanach 1970; Charlesworth 1985; Fukazawa 1983; Keatinge 1912, 1921; R. Kumar 1968; Mann 1917; Mann and Kanitkar 1921; McAlpin 1983; Perlin 1978.

simply consists of the description and codification of existing knowledge, with periodic insertions concerning new alternatives. Thus, in the 1882 tract, a brief section on the use of animal manure notes that farmers, knowing the virtues of cattle dung, already use it as manure, but that they are unaware of the method already established in England (*vilāyat*) for using the urine of cattle to produce fertilizer. But what is important is that the entire scheme of agricultural knowledge is beginning to be transformed into a seamless web of technical information, where the line between what farmers already know (and thus do not need to be told) and what they do not know is increasingly obscure. This transformation of practical knowledge into agronomy is the critical symptom, at the level of discourse, of the process of commercialization.

One strand of the tract literature of the latter part of the nineteenth century (exemplified by K. Khare 1882) is fundamentally populist, anti-moneylender and pro-farmer, in its tone. It is only secondarily technical and agronomic in its rhetoric, and to the extent that the world of commerce (*vyāpār*) enters its framework, it is largely in terms of the relationships between moneylenders and farmers. In this model, farmers are presented as toiling, poor, ignorant, and exploited, whereas the landlord/moneylender (often portrayed ethnically as a *marvadi* or *baniya*, members of business communities with their origins in Gujarat and Rajasthan) is seen as avaricious, literate, calculating, heartless. Though the farmer, in this type of rhetoric, is exhorted about the virtues of work (*udyōg*), utility (*fāydā, lābh*), and organized leisure (*vishrānti*), he is still not conceived fundamentally as an entrepreneur. Indeed, in this work, farming (*shēthi karṇyā*) and commerce (*vyāpār*) are contrasting activities, and the farmer (*shētkari*) and the moneylender (*sāvkār*) are seen in a nasty but unavoidable symbiosis. It is in the context of ameliorating, but not transforming, this relationship that the language of commerce enters this tract, in the terminology of loans (*karja*), interest (*vyāj*), amounts (*rakkam*), security for loans (*vasūl*), and so on. The sole use of the term *bhāṇdval* (capital) in this text is with reference to moneylenders. Although this does not mean that farmers in Maharashtra in the 1880s were not involved in commercial agriculture, it does suggest that the conception of farmers as capitalists (*bhāṇdvaldār*) was still alien to much official discourse.

But in the 1890 tract by Apte, called *The Best Farmer* (*Uttama Shētkari*), the romantic and populist tone of the earlier tracts gives way to a more businesslike, technical, and specialized treatment. This work is a careful analysis of the relationship between farm size, hired labor, and landowners' participation in agriculture, with a fairly complex conception of the optimization of various forms of owner-laborer relationships.

This text is also a very early index of the emergence of time as a commercialized resource in agriculture. Early in the text, it is asserted that the value (*mōl*) of time (*vēḷ*) in agriculture is matched in very few other businesses (*vyāpār*), and a whole series of examples is provided of how various contingencies tend to interfere with the proper timing of agricultural activities and thus cause loss (*nuksān, thōtā*) to the farmer. Notable in this picture of the exigencies of timing is the failure to mention man-made water problems (though uncertain rainfall is mentioned) and the implication that ritual obligations generally take (and ought to take) precedence over agricultural pressures.

So too, agricultural produce is referred to in the text as *māl* (goods) and there is an implicit sense of the profitability of rural enterprise underlying the examples in the text. Thus a farmer who owns a "one-pair" holding (i.e., what can be worked by a pair of bullocks, roughly equal to 16–20 acres) by himself with the assistance of careless casual laborers, is likely not to be doing very well, even if he looks to the outside observer as if he is very wealthy. The small farmer (*lahāṇ shēth karṇārā*—itself probably a recent technical category in this official discourse), is seen as lacking cash capital (*paishāchā bhāṇḍval*). He is depicted as suffering from being on the wrong side of a series of economies of scale and thus as perennially a victim of the scarcity of cash (*paishāchī taṇchāi*).

This 1890 text represents a strong pitch for partnership and sharing arrangements (*bhāgīdāri, sarkati*) among small farmers, and in this context what emerges is a fully fledged conception of agricultural capital. It is explicitly noted that cash is not the only form of capital (*bhāṇḍval*) required for farming, but that the seeds, animal feed, tools for weeding, cultivating, threshing, etc. are also forms of capital. Partnerships are seen as a way to accumulate larger capital and large capital enterprises are said to involve lower costs (*mōtyā bhāṇḍvalāchē vyāpārāth kharcha kamī lāgtō*). Furthermore, the larger the capital, the greater the profit (*jitkē bhāṇḍval moṭhē titka fāydā mōṭhā*). The virtues of the division of labor (*shrama-vibhāga*) are seen as an adjunct to the idea of partnerships in small-scale farming.

In general, this tract is dominated by a full-blown conception of farming as a capital-oriented business and of the virtues of "economizing," particularly from the point of view of partnerships among small farmers. What is notable is that even in this tract, wells are not seen as a major focus of cooperative control or ownership, and are largely taken for granted as aspects of the agrarian landscape. The sole form in which problems of water are mentioned is in terms of the uncertainty of rainfall, as in the earlier tracts.

Thus, by 1890, it appears that a mature agronomic discourse in Marathi had emerged, largely formulated by petty officials in the bureaucracy. The samples we have looked at allow us to see the formation of a rudimentary commercial consciousness in agronomic discourse. However, these tracts seem even in 1890 to conceive of agriculture as largely a social process, in which farmers and farming are part of a larger world of relations, groups, and orientations. It is not yet a technical or narrowly scientific discourse, devoid of social analysis, political opinions, or cultural polemics.

Before turning to a contemporary example of official agronomic discourse, exemplified by a farmer's diary from 1981, it is important to note that the period from 1890 to 1980 is obviously one which involved major social, economic, and technical transformations in the rural landscape of Maharashtra. Though it is far outside the scope of this chapter even to summarize these changes, the most important among them must be noted: the rapid expansion of cultivation in the period from 1880 to 1920, which has some of the marks of a boom period: rising prices for agricultural commodities, increased productivity, absorption of most arable land and water resources. This period was followed by a slump which lasted well into the 1930s worldwide, during which there was little significant growth. But starting in the 1940s, and continuing up to the time of writing (late 1980s), we have had the beginnings of a major technological revolution in agriculture, the key features of which are the availability and spread of chemical fertilizers, new varieties of seeds, mechanized tools for a variety of agricultural operations, and oil and electricity as new sources of power. This agricultural revolution, it must be stressed, has not spread very deeply into rural society in Maharashtra, but it clearly indicates the technological shape of things to come.

The *Farmer's Diary* (*Krishival Dāyiri*, edited by H. L. Nipunge) for 1981 (which combines the features of an American-style farmer's almanac with those of a daily notebook and record) was produced by a publishing house in Pune to be sold at a price of Rs 10, a little over one US dollar at the then current rate of exchange, but a significant sum of money for any but the richest farmers. The content of the diary as well as its price indicate clearly that it was directed at the uppermost stratum of Maharashtra's farmers. It consists of almost 170 pages of small-print text, which precede a rather small number of blank entry pages for the days of the year. The printed text, which is heavily interspersed with advertisements for seed, fertilizer, and farm machinery companies, is an extremely detailed and technical guide to every important aspect of "progressive" or "modern" (*ādhūnik*) farming in Maharashtra. As such, it doubtlessly represents the vocabulary that is shared by agricultural colleges, agribusiness, and agricultural extension workers in today's Maharashtra. Coming almost one hundred years after the 1890 tract I discussed earlier, a century characterized by steady growth in agricultural education as well as in agribusiness, it is no surprise that this text takes the commercial logic and structure of agriculture wholly for granted, and focuses largely on the technical and agronomic specifics of soils, seeds, modern cultivation techniques, water, and fertilizer use for a large variety of commercial crops. It has a chapter each devoted to sugarcane and to onions, both important commercial crops in Maharashtra, and others devoted to fruits, flowers, modern machinery, seeds, and fertilizer. Throughout, there is an emphasis on the use of newly developed hybrids as well as on the use of a wide variety of chemical fertilizers. Though a great deal could be said about the vocabulary and ethos of the agronomic discourse contained in this text, I will restrict myself to a few points which are salient to the larger argument of this chapter.

The most striking feature of this text is the virtual elimination of rough measurement algorithms, and their replacement by extremely precise (generally Western) measures. Whether it is a question of the depth of the water table, the amount of fertilizer appropriate to various crops, the number of times a particular crop needs to be watered, the average yields of crops in the state, or anything else, the text generally gives precise numerical measures. It therefore represents the culmination of a process of technical and commercial penetration of indigenous agricultural discourse, which, as I will show in a subsequent section, depended mostly on approximate, relational, and context-bound kinds of measurement. If we look back at the earlier tracts from this perspective, we can see that in 1852 this type of precise idiom of measure was virtually absent; it begins to appear in the 1882 and 1890 tracts, although even in these the more approximate and practice-oriented forms of measure tend to coexist with the new, more technical forms. But by 1981 it is clear that indigenous agronomic discourse has no room for approximate or context-tied forms of measurement.

The second notable fact is that the entire framework of this 1981 text is profoundly individualistic. There is no indication anywhere in it that there are complex forms of cooperation and interdependence in rural

Maharashtra, both between wealthier farmers, and between them and poorer farmers. In this sense, not only can we see how the entrepreneurial, individualistic ethos sets the tone of mature agronomic discourse, but also that as such discourse grows more technical, it tends by its nature to become less sociological. Put another way, by 1981 agronomic discourse ceases to have any concern with agrarian relations and sees farming as a wholly technical enterprise.

Similarly, in this text, the rural calendar has become wholly demystified and all sense of the ritual periodicities that frame agricultural activity has been eliminated. Although the tripartite terminology for the climatic seasons (*unhāḷā, pāvsāḷa, hivāḷa*) and the dual structure of the cropping seasons (*kharif, rabi*) is still in place, the major change is that the folk organization of major agricultural activities according to the system of *nakshatras* (lunar asterisms) is completely eliminated; instead the English calendar months and then various numbers of days to characterize the time between operations are used. The earlier tracts all refer to the *nakshatras* as ways to time major operations, as do farmers in Vadi and elsewhere in Maharashtra today. More important (and anticipating the discussion in the next section of the chapter), the text as a whole clearly sees agricultural activity as the driving force of the calendar, as exhaustive in its temporal claims, and as wholly independent of ritual and other social periodicities. This text truly instantiates what, paraphrasing E. P. Thompson (1967), we might call agronomic time.

In a chapter on bank loans, the text makes it clear that the only loans that are relevant are those that are meant for the improvement (*sudhārnā*) of the farm and for increased production (*utpādan vaḍhisāṭhi*). This is the only context in which the text brings up the digging of new wells or the deepening of old ones, among examples of purposes for which banks are likely to grant loans. The text also makes it clear that banks are not interested in loans for consumption needs, and warns farmers not to divert the money they receive for improved agricultural production to immediate consumption needs. In general, the section on bank loans confirms the overall tone of the text, which is that of a technical manual for the exemplary (*ādarsh*) farmer, committed to new techniques and crops, oriented principally to the marketplace, free of the social relations of rural life and the rhythms of the ritual calendar. Such a figure is clearly not yet a reality in rural Maharashtra, but he is the model target (and ideological goal) of the new agronomy.

This brief sketch of change in the discourse of agriculture in Maharashtra was meant to complement our knowledge of changes "on the ground" in the last century. But it also puts us in a better position to interpret and place in context the very specific shifts in practice and ideology that I shall discuss next, this time in the setting of a single village. Today, as in the past, rural Maharashtra is characterized by extreme spatial differentiation (Charlesworth 1985: 142–55), both in ecology and in the resulting patterns of commercialization and social differentiation, so that there can be sharp differences not only between broad regions within the state, within districts, and within *talukas* (subdivisions), but even between villages which are a few miles from each other. One cannot therefore leap easily from macro- to micro-data, but the account I have given of the formation of a regional agronomic discourse can serve as a general backdrop for the specific case I turn to now.

The Ethnographic Locus

The village from which I have drawn this data—and to which I have given the pseudonym Vadi—is located about 25 miles southeast of the city of Pune, in Purandhar *taluka* (subdivision), Pune district, about 130 miles inland from the coastal metropolis of Mumbai. Its location places it on a gradient of decreasing rainfall in the Deccan Plateau. Rainfall in Vadi probably totals less than 25 inches in most years, and is sharply seasonal. The peak period of rainfall in normal years is in the months of June, July, August, and September, which account for about 75 percent of this total. October and November usually account for about 15 percent, the months from December to March for about 3 percent, and April and May for about 7 percent. These figures are very approximate, for there can be sharp year-to-year fluctuations from this norm. The village is about 2.5 miles from Saswad, the *taluka* headquarters, which is the principal bus link to Pune and to Mumbai. There is a road passing the village which is used by the buses of the State Transport system and by the trucks of the transport companies that move vegetables from villages like Vadi to Pune and to Mumbai.

The population of Vadi in 1981 consisted of approximately 900 persons, who were distributed in 193 households. About 30 percent of these households contained families that were "joint" (*ēkatra*) in one or another sense, while the remaining 70 percent were "nuclear" (*vibhakta*). The total amount of cultivated land was about 880 acres of which about 280 acres (less than 33 percent) was wet land, i.e., land that has access to water above and beyond rainwater. Mean landholdings were 4.5 acres, with mean dry landholdings being 3.1 acres and mean wet landholdings being 1.4 acres.

Vadi has a very significant set of links with the outside world. Out of the 193 households, 104 had one (and often more) members of the family outside the village, usually earning a living in Mumbai or Pune. But this should not give the impression that Vadi is a "remittance" economy in any simple sense, since many of these wage earners support dependents in the city, and others, for a variety of reasons, send cash back to the village only in special circumstances. Thus it is no surprise that although 104 households had working members outside Vadi, only 33 of these households described cash salaries as their principal means of subsistence (when compared with income from cash crops, sale of family labor, and the products of their own fields).

The caste composition of Vadi was relatively simple. Out of the total of 193 households, 174 were Maratha, and the rest were distributed among the various lower service castes, including some considered "untouchable." When villagers stated that this was a "Maratha" village, they were not far wrong. The Maratha households themselves were organized into four numerically dominant lineages (*bhāuki*) and three numerically minor ones. The families in each lineage shared surnames (*āḍnāv*), although there is here an ethnographic curiosity in that two of the dominant Maratha lineages share the same *āḍnāv*. The families of the other castes were similarly identifiable by shared surnames.

I have already noted that mean landholdings were small. Agriculture, to produce crops for household consumption as well as for sale, was the principal economic activity of the villagers. The principal subsistence crops were sorghum (*jowar*) and millet (*bajri*), and most villagers grew at least some of each. In addition, however, there was a very large number of other cultivars. Small amounts of wheat and rice were grown. The principal commercial crops were sugarcane, onions, and green peas. Also important, but more for consumption than for sale, were a variety of lentils and pulses, peanuts, many kinds of greens, and small amounts of tomatoes, carrots, figs, fodder, grass, and flowers. All the crops grown principally for sale (and here peas and onions are the most important), as well as the vegetables grown for home consumption, required irrigated land.

There are two major cropping seasons: the *kharif* season, from June to October (which relies on the monsoon rains) and the *rabi* (or winter) season, when the bulk of the irrigation-dependent, market-oriented farming is done, which runs from November to February. The hot (*uṇhāḷā*) season from March to May is the most taxing because of the heat and lack of water, but those who did have access to water in this season used it to grow certain vegetables. The hot season is also the season for repair of tools, preparation of the land in anticipation of the June rains, and the celebration of marriages and other village festivities. It is the season of high expenditure and low income for many households.

While the technology of agriculture was largely traditional, its economic framework was no longer so traditional. The bullock and the plow were still the key instruments of agriculture, and the tools used for winnowing, weeding, reaping, sowing, threshing, and harvesting were still largely part of a very ancient material inventory.[4] Yet there had been important changes. The use of fertilizer and of pesticides, particularly for cash crops, had become common, and animal manure was infrequently used. Agricultural labor was paid for almost entirely in cash, and there were clearly understood rates of payment for different tasks, seasons, and genders. Vadi was a labor-surplus village, for though there were very few landless households, the number of land-poor households was quite large. Even the intermittent flow of urban remittances was inadequate to sustain the land-poor households, whose women and men had to sell their labor in addition to using it to manage their own smallholdings. Thus it was not often that the farmers of Vadi needed to hire laborers from other villages.

Vadi, in 1981–82, was in a variety of ways highly monetized. Even the poorest households were deeply tied into the cash nexus and most households, in the opinion of these farmers, would have collapsed without a few hundred rupees per month, at the very least (Rs 9 = US $1 then). One major way to improve one's position in a world dominated by

---

4.   The whole topic of changes in agricultural technology in Western India needs careful examination of a sort that has yet to be given to it. But it is highly probable that the major technological break, prior to the recent increase in heavy machinery, new seed varieties, fertilizer, and irrigation technology, is the incorporation of metal into what were previously wholly wooden farm implements. Though this shift doubtlessly began in the nineteenth century, there is some evidence that it took off only in the early part of this century under the stimulation of agribusiness and rural commercial interests: see Mann and Kanitkar 1921. As far as wells are concerned, the shift from earthen to masonry walls probably occurred in two waves, the first in the 1850s and the second in the period from 1880 to 1920, as responses to commercial opportunities in the first case and to government loan programs in the second.

cash transactions was to enter the market in agricultural commodities, not only as a laborer (where the prospects for improvement were dismal) but as a producer. This meant gaining access, however precariously, to irrigated land. Before I can discuss local changes in agricultural knowledge in the context of commercialization, it is essential to present the elementary facts surrounding irrigated agriculture in Vadi.

The Technology and Sociology of Irrigation in Vadi

The basic technological structure of the 74 wells in use in Vadi in 1981–82 probably goes back at least a millennium and consists of a hole dug in the soil to a depth of anything from 20 to 60 feet (about 6 to 18 meters), and with a diameter of anything from 15 to 30 feet (3 to 9 meters).[5] The traditional measure for the depth of a well is a *paras* or *purush*, indicating the height of an adult male, but actually equivalent to about 7 feet (2 meters). Although some wells were probably dug by family or village labor, specialist castes of well-diggers are a well-known part of the historical record in Western and Southern India. In the past, the inner walls of this hole were "finished" with stone and lime, and there would have been a wooden superstructure. This superstructure would permit the dropping and lifting of a leather water container. The raising and lifting would have been accomplished by either two or four bullocks.

By the 1970s, wells had acquired some new features, though their basic design persists. Cement had largely replaced lime for the finishing of the interior; steel containers (*mōṭ*) had replaced the leather water containers; and, in a few cases, rented boring machines had replaced human labor for the actual digging. Most important, animal power had come to be regarded as obsolete, although about 12 wells still used this form of power. The energy source of choice was electricity, although about 5 wells were powered by diesel engines. This meant that there were about 57 wells that were powered by 3 or 5 hp electric motors.

Sometimes these modernized wells had varying lengths of pipeline, but often traditional dug channels (*pat*) were used to take the water from the mouth of the well to the fields. Most wells physically predated the arrival of electricity, and were thus simply electrified traditional

---

5.   This discussion of wells draws heavily on Appadurai 1984c: 3–14 [chapter 3 in this volume].

open-surface wells. The technology of wells may thus better be called mixed than traditional.

Wells were part of the picture of very small and fragmented holdings in Vadi, but were also indicative of a relatively high proportion (33 percent) of irrigated land to total cultivated land, compared to the figure for the state, which was 11 percent in 1975–76. In Vadi, in 1981, 142 households shared about 280 acres of wet land. Of these households, about 33 percent had wet landholdings of less than 1 acre, about 60 percent had less than 2 acres, and about 80 percent had less than 3 acres. Only 11 of these households had more than 5 irrigated acres each, and 1 of these had 25 acres, the largest concentration of wet landholdings in Vadi. I present these figures to show that these irrigated holdings are extremely modest, by and large.

Most farmers owned several plots (*tukḍē*) of wet land; these holdings were not usually physically contiguous, which means that the farmers were often shareholders (*hissēdār, vātekārī*) in more than one well. Although there were 24 single-owner wells, and 13 two-owner wells, even the farmers involved in these had shares in some of the other wells, which had co-sharers ranging in number from 3 to the most involuted case, which involved 31 co-sharers. The scattered picture of individual landholdings was further layered over by a crisscrossing web of shares in wells. Shares in wells usually remained attached to the pieces of land with which they were associated and, in Vadi, to buy or inherit a piece of land was by definition to inherit a share in the well which allowed it to be irrigated. Yet shares in wells were not entirely tied to pieces of land for wells could fall into disuse; or water from one well (theoretically meant to irrigate a particular plot) could be diverted by the shareholder to another plot not associated with it; or well shares could lie dormant while the pieces of land associated with them were watered by water from another well to which the shareholder had access.

Nevertheless, as a rule, shares in wells were closely associated with pieces of land, and thus the major way in which shareholders in wells acquired these holdings was through land inherited from their male parents. This is reflected in the fact that many wells had shareholders who were all male agnates (paternal kinsmen) from the same named lineage, and sometimes they were sons of the same father. This picture of patrilineally inherited shares was fairly persistent, so that when one encountered a well which had mixed lineage membership, or in which there was one anomalous surname, it could easily be traced to one of the following three sources: a sale of the land (and the associated well share) to an outsider by a lineage member in financial difficulty; the acquisition of a piece of lineage land by an outsider because of a loan default in which the land was the security (*tāraṇ*); or, in the few cases where a woman was named as a shareholder, it turned out that she was a widowed member of the lineage, whose husband had received that land as part of her dowry, with the land reverting to her after his death.

Approximately 33 percent of these wells had between 1 and 4 shareholders and thus did not require complex systems for sharing water. But the remaining 66 percent, which had between 5 and 31 shareholders, did require complex time-sharing systems. To understand these systems, it is necessary to have some knowledge of the role of wells in agricultural production. Well-watered land is (and has been for the known past) crucial to growing most crops in the winter and summer seasons when the rains are minimal. Very few wells had water through all 12 months, and it is these few 12-month wells (*bārāmāhi*) that allowed their beneficiaries to grow sugarcane, which requires ample water throughout the year. The bulk of wells were known as 8-month wells (*āṭmahi*), and yielded water from approximately mid-June to mid-February. Such 8-month wells permitted the growing of onions and green peas (the two major cash crops), plus a variety of other vegetables and fruits which were grown both for market and for home consumption, as well as small amounts of rice and wheat.

In wells that had more than four or five shareholders, who were working small plots of land and growing the same cash crops (such as onions) at much the same times, there were fairly complex turn-taking (*pāḷi*) systems. These systems varied depending on the number of shareholders, the water retention capabilities of the well, especially in the hot weather, the crops being grown by the shareholders, and the amount of land under the well in question. Usually the system was a twelve-day or eight-day rotation, and the amount of time (one day or two days or a part of a day) that a particular turn consisted of depended on the amount of land that a particular landholder had in his share. It was in the hot season, when the water level dropped, and when the cash crops needed water in order to yield profits, that these systems came into play. It was also at these times that those farmers who had access to their own wells or to low-membership wells had the greatest advantage.

In general, partly because of the fragmented holdings under wells and the problem of low capital for many of these farmers, few wells involved one hundred percent use of the plots that were described as being "under" them (*vihīrīkhāḷī*). Frequently, only a third of the acreage nominally associated with the well was actually in productive use. This was a sign of the incapacity of shareholders to afford the labor and other costs associated with full use of their well-linked acreage. In most cases, the underutilization of these nominally irrigated plots was a function of these disabilities and not of the limits of the wells alone. Consolidation of holdings is the key to the economics of using these wells optimally, but most farmers had holdings that were far from each other in addition to being small. Wealthier farmers were always seeking to acquire, either by direct purchase or by mortgage defaults, plots near ones they already owned.

All farmers in Vadi who lacked access to shares in wells would have liked to acquire such shares. All farmers with shares would have liked to see these shares electrified. (I speak of electrified "shares" rather than of electrified wells because there were several cases of wells in which some shareholders had invested in motors which they operated during their turns. The motor was not available to other shareholders who could not afford to participate in the original investment, and who therefore used bullock power during their turns or, in a few cases, rented diesel engines, which were portable.) And all farmers would have liked to have wells of their own, preferably electrified, without having to cooperate with other farmers in the original investment or in the subsequent turn-taking. The reasons for this antipathy towards partnership, in a community tradi- tionally committed to the value of sociality, are discussed in the conclu- sion to this chapter.

The motorized wells which had multiple shareholders clearly reflect- ed the fact that the costs of electrification (a 3 hp motor cost about Rs 5,000 [US \$555] and a 5 hp motor about Rs 8,000 [US \$888] in 1981) exceeded the financial capabilities of most farmers. Yet the decision to invest jointly in a new well was even harder than the decision to invest jointly in a new motor for an existing well. The costs of a new well, in- cluding digging it, installing a motor, and perhaps installing pipeline, ranged from Rs 20,000 (US \$2,222) to Rs 40,000 (US \$4,444). This was a very sizeable investment, since the mean annual cash income of most small farmers (from all sources) was unlikely to exceed Rs 5,000. Given the small individual plots, the chances that some of the co-sharers would not be able to afford the inputs to make the optimal use of the irrigated land, and the chances that economic difficulties would make some of them renege on their share of the bank loan repayments or the electric- ity bills, it was no surprise that all but one of the new wells dug in the five years before 1981 were entrepreneurial ventures by single farmers.

There had been joint efforts to electrify existing wells, but there were several wells where plans to electrify had not come to fruition, and others that, though electrified, were underutilized, especially by the poorer shareholders.

Knowledge Shifts in the Locality

Let us recollect, at this point, the argument about epistemological change which was previewed in the introduction to this chapter. It was suggested that the commercialization of agriculture in the last century has created a new agronomic episteme, which renders much of the existing agrarian techne obsolete. Through a series of examples, three of which pertain to the content of knowledge, and three others to styles of knowledge, I shall demonstrate how commercialization leads to radical epistemological shifts.

Knowledge Loss

First, very soon knowledge of how to construct, maintain, and efficiently operate nonmotorized wells will become obsolete, just as knowledge about leather water containers has already largely vanished because of their replacement by metal water containers in wells. Why should we worry about the loss of this particular sort of knowledge? After all, it might be claimed, animal-powered traditional wells belong to an inefficient and rapidly disappearing mode, and it is likely (as well as desirable) that more and more farmers will acquire shares in motorized wells or in larger modern systems of water distribution. Is it not simply urban romanticism about rural life to regret the passing of such knowledge?

The fact of the matter is that in many dry parts of rural India, like Maharashtra, a significant number of farmers still eke out their subsistence on the edge of commercial agriculture by their access to bullock-drawn well water. For them the understanding of the requirements and uses of such wells is by no means irrelevant. Secondly, for many farmers, participation in the ownership of electric motors for well water is a risky matter, and sometimes partnerships in such wells fail, or, due to economic exigencies, shares in such wells have to be sold. In these cases, those without access to, and knowledge of, traditional techniques are likely to be pushed out of the market in cash crops (which require irrigation) completely. This will make the ups and downs of farm fortunes sharper in the current transitional milieu. Thus, until such time as there is universal and reliable access to electric power for wells, knowledge of bullock-drawn well water ought not to be pushed into obsolescence. Finally, insofar as bullock-powered wells often involve bullock-sharing systems, which draw poorer farmers into partnership arrangements, the elimination of these systems also means the end of certain modes of co-operation among farmers. Again, until it is perfectly clear that all farmers operate in a world in which household autonomy is a safe and satisfying mode of organizing subsistence, such changes are risky ways of eating into social capital, particularly for poorer farmers.

As for the shift from leather to metal water containers, the argument is simpler. This shift pushes farmers inexorably towards greater dependence on large-scale markets, and towards greater vulnerability to price shifts and uncertainties in supply. If ever there is a major change in prices for metal goods, a great many poorer farmers are likely to find themselves going deeper into debt in order to afford metal water containers. Further, since the making of leather water containers was an important occupational entitlement of the lowest leather-working castes, this change pushes them into metropolitan markets for their goods and services, thus further compromising the autonomy of rural economies.

Second, with increased dependence on industrially produced fertilizers, even among small farmers, detailed knowledge about how best to use animal manure for agricultural production will become restricted to an older generation and will then disappear. Again, why should we care? First, because in such complex traditional ecosystems, with their delicate relationships between animal manure, agricultural productivity, costs of farming, relative local self-sufficiency, and impact on the soil, there is ample evidence that animal manure can be extremely effective when available. The problem in the part of Maharashtra in which I worked is that in the last serious period of drought, in 1972, a great many cattle were sold, and local cattle populations have never returned to their previous levels. When this situation is combined with the sort of pressure on farmers from government, agribusiness, and outside experts to shift to industrial fertilizers (a part of the growing agronomic episteme I described in the third section of this chapter), we can see why farmers, even smaller ones, might be tempted to abandon the use of animal manure, and the knowledge of the algorithms traditionally associated with its use. Among many farmers, the pressure to generate sizeable short-term cash incomes (to meet subsistence needs that can increasingly be met only with cash) leads to over-use of chemical fertilizers, with possibly disastrous long-term effects on the soil. In Maharashtra, as elsewhere in India, there is a widespread feeling that chemical fertilizers "heat" the soil excessively. Thus, in abandoning older fertilizing technologies, farmers are losing the capability to fall back on a technology that might, in certain circumstances, be better for them and their fields. Knowledge lost, in the case of agricultural techniques, is choice foregone.

Third, as reliance on government geologists and other modern experts for locating subsurface water sources increases, there is going to be reduced demand for the services of water-diviners. In rural Maharashtra, such individuals, called *pānhāḍi*, are frequently drawn upon in the course of decisions to locate new wells. Whatever the objective virtues of their systems for divining the location of subsurface water (and I, for one, have an open mind on this question), they serve an important role in contemporary decisions to sink wells. Sinking a new well, in the parts of rural Maharashtra with which I am familiar, is a costly, risky, and time-consuming process. It involves the commitment of major household resources, often the contracting of partnership ties with other local farmers, the taking on of debts to banks or cooperatives, and the commitment of a large and indefinite amount of family time for the supervision of whoever does the actual work. Given the nature of the costs and the potential benefits, it is a major decision and one attended with considerable anxiety. A crucial part of the decision is the question of where to locate the well. Farmers themselves have projections, based on village understandings, the location of other wells (old and new), and the advice of friends and neighbors, about where there is likely to be a good vein. Government geologists, who use Western scientific techniques and instruments, have a different conception of the water table and of the optimal places for a well on any given plot of land. So far, farmers have been able to arrive at what they regard as reliable decisions in this crucial matter by triangulating these three kinds of knowledge and then arriving at a choice which best conforms with the predictions of either two or all three of these modes. As the expertise of water-diviners disappears, it is not just that we lose an important traditional eco-technical skill. We also lose one component in a process which allows farmers to make a complex and risky decision using multiple diagnoses. Here again, a loss in knowledge is a curtailment in epistemological multiplicity and choice.

What is true of material technologies is less true of ecological knowledge. Farmers' knowledge about rainfall, soil, and water as natural systems seems to have survived in many parts of India, but it is only a matter of time before reliance on radio, television, and other metropolitan forms of agrarian expertise pushes indigenous knowledge increasingly out of the picture. What is, of course, most resilient is knowledge about people, deities, cosmological happenings, and ritual calendars and rhythms. In this area the fabric of traditional rural knowledge seems to have been least affected. Still, since knowledge, especially in rural settings, is not tightly compartmentalized, the archive as a whole will probably begin to be structurally transformed, although it is difficult to say how or when.

Shifts in Ways of Knowing

I have spoken so far about the content or archive of agricultural knowledge. In this regard, I have suggested, change is fairly rapid and fairly extensive. But what about the traditional way of knowing, traditional rural epistemology? In the third section above I have already suggested some of the significant ways in which the emerging agronomic discourse of the last century redefined the world of the farmer. In particular, I pointed out ways in which the terminology of measurement and the handling of time were altered by the incipient commercial setting. In what follows, I locate these shifts in the specifics of the farming world of Vadi, and in its *epistemological style*. This style, in any community, has several dimensions, of which the following three are especially important: (1) typical modes of assessing certain phenomena, what we might call *modes of analysis*; (2) typical ways in which knowledge is shared or distributed in the community, i.e., *the political economy of expertise* in that community; and (3) the strategic *relationship between sectors of knowledge* (and thus of experience), which determines what kind of knowledge takes priority over what other kind. This last dimension is where matters of knowledge shade over most visibly into matters of value. I turn now to some examples of each of these dimensions of the epistemological style of farmers in Vadi, and changes to which they provide testimony.

Using material from Maharashtra, I have suggested in chapter 1 [of this volume] that the difference between contemporary Western terminologies of measurement and their non-Western, rural counterparts is not simply a difference in vocabularies, calling for care in translation. Rather, rural terminologies of measurement reveal assumptions about the relationship between number and quantity, the relationship between measures and standards, the acceptability of approximation over precision, and the centrality of social negotiation to measurement, which are fundamentally divergent from the abstract, context-free, precise norms to which contemporary scientific systems aspire. Thus, when farmers assess the extent of their lands, their yields, their local populations and subpopulations, their needs, and many other things, they do so in terms which are not just superficially different from our own but which contain and reflect a very different understanding of what measurement is all about.

One example of this important difference will have to suffice here. Farmers engaged in growing onions (largely for the market) often have to buy onion seedlings from other farmers. When the purchase of these seedlings is negotiated, it is done in terms of a measure called a *vāfā*, a roughly standardized "bed" in which such seedlings are planted. The buyer bids a certain sum for a particular *vāfā* (or set of *vāfā*) of seedlings, and then there may be a counteroffer by the seller, and then a final resolution. Although this may look like standard haggling over the price (i.e., the value) of a clear-cut amount of something, it is rather negotiation over the amount itself, expressed in the idiom of price. Since these "beds" vary in size and shape and since the number of seedlings in them has to be guessed at visually, what in effect the buyer and seller are bargaining over is their respective estimates of quantity using the measure of price—offers and counteroffers. Such relationships between quantity estimates, approximation, and value characterize many other sorts of activities in rural Maharashtra.

Yet, in a world which is increasingly defined by money, by markets, and by externally calibrated institutions of measurement, such as clocks, calendars, and measuring tapes, a very different mode of measuring is becoming relevant to more and more contexts in rural life. This new mode is characterized by precise and context-free instruments of measure, nonnegotiable results of acts of measurement, and a generalized replacement of approximation by precision. Signs of this shift are everywhere, though the traditional mode of measuring is still the normal one. But every farmer who operates with cash flows, who works in industrial or quasi-industrial settings, and who responds to bureaucratic requirements in his search for cash, credit, electricity, or health needs must learn new ways to measure his world, or at least to express his estimates of things. Again this sort of erosion of traditional modes of analysis is not just unfortunate in itself, but reflects the degree to which farmers (often in spite of their preferences) are forced into large-scale, metropolitan interactions, contexts, and modes of thought. To the degree that such incorporation into larger systems is neither pleasant nor freely chosen, its accompanying epistemological costs must, in principle, be deemed high.

As regards the political economy of expertise, it is possible to postulate a growing unevenness in the distribution of agricultural knowledge, both within and across specific agricultural communities and regions. The intensification of agriculture has among its many consequences the spatial and social differentiation remarked on by Charlesworth (1985) and others. Increasingly, there are crops (such as sugarcane) which demand that plots be given over to them permanently and regions that are constrained to specialize in this or that crop because of market pressures and opportunities. There are farmers who specialize in this or that crop. The crudest example of this last factor is that in more and more communities, there is a clear gap between those wealthier farmers whose lands are completely (or largely) given over to commercial crops and those whose small plots are devoted mainly to subsistence crops.

Of course, this growing differentiation does not have direct implications for the distribution of knowledge, since poorer farmers often work on the commercial plots of richer farmers and richer farmers maintain portions of their land for subsistence crops so as to be free of the vagaries of the market. Yet there is no doubt that knowledge of agricultural operations is now more intricately shared, especially in regard to the overall strategic handling of livelihood. The agronomic discourse discussed earlier is not evenly distributed in Vadi. Wealthier farmers today speak the language of risk (*khatrā*), of investment (*kharcha*), of capital (*bhāṇdval*), and of planning (*vichār*) in ways that reflect directly their exposure to, and interest in, the discourse of fertilizer companies, bank officials, large agricultural traders, and development experts, both public and private. The 1981 farmer's diary discussed earlier epitomizes this type of usage. Poorer farmers, by contrast, though they will occasionally speak of capital, *nafā-thōtā* (profit and loss), and so on, are not active or frequent users of the language of agricultural entrepreneurship.

These linguistic variations reflect deeper and subtler variations in how knowledge is shared. It seems clear that, over a long period of time, the amount, at the level of knowledge, of what Anthony Wallace called the replication of uniformity or Durkheim would have called mechanical solidarity has decreased; and there is more and more of what Wallace called the organization of diversity and Durkheim would have called organic solidarity (Wallace 1970; Durkheim 1960). In short, farmers increasingly know what they know in a piecemeal manner, consonant with technical and environmental segmentation as well as with social and economic stratification. More and more rural communities are held together because of differences—rather than through similarities—in what various persons and groups know about the conduct of agriculture. Needless to say, such unevenness can and does reinforce structures of inequality and domination in rural India. Though this tendency too is not yet dominant, its direction is clear. It is towards that division of epistemological labor which characterizes complex modern communities the world over.

The strategic relationship between sectors of knowledge is the hardest aspect of the epistemological style of rural communities to pin down, but it is perhaps the most important. In any given epistemological universe, some things frame others, some things are regarded as less questionable than others, some issues and perspectives color the way others are apprehended, discussed, and acted upon. It is this aspect of any particular system of knowing and speaking that Michel Foucault sought to capture in his idea of a discursive formation (Hoy 1986).

One major shift that is underway in the discursive formation of rural India, again based on my fieldwork in Vadi, concerns the experience and handling of the temporal dimension of rural experience. Time is a central resource in all agricultural communities, and India is no exception. Time is experienced as the continuing interaction of several kinds of rhythms and periodicities, cosmological, ecological, ritual, and economic. The timing of agricultural decisions reflects very complex negotiations and compromises between these various kinds of periodicities, and I have elsewhere argued that poorer farmers are at a very specific kind of disadvantage in the distribution of time as an agricultural resource.[6]

But I want here to make a more general point. While it appears that in the past ritual and ecological periodicities set the rhythms of production, consumption, and reproduction, and defined the framework of knowledge and of belief within which production goals were set and pursued (all the nineteenth-century tracts discussed earlier support this view), this practical and epistemological priority is in the process of being reversed. Increasingly, as suggested earlier, time itself is subject to the overwhelming pressure of the marketplace and the logic of commercialization. That is, more and more of the rhythm of agricultural life is set by the labor, cash, and climatic needs of commercial crops, affecting not only those wealthier farmers who are massively tied to markets in agricultural commodities, but also those poorer farmers who provide the labor and part of the clientele for the products of this intensification and commercialization of agriculture. As I suggested earlier, the logic of agronomic time is beginning to make increasingly involved a limited

---

6.   This important topic has not been paid much attention by students of agrarian life in South Asia; an important exception is Amin 1982.

social calendar, to set the pace of life, and to leave ritual and ecological periodicities in a somewhat more marginalized role.

Let me explain by means of an ethnographic example. The main commercial crops in this part of western Maharashtra are sugarcane, onions, and peas. In general, these crops have been inserted into a cropping cycle which was previously dominated by the cultivation of sorghum and millet in two long seasons (monsoon and winter), with a low-activity hot season between them. In this situation, not only was there greater temporal slack during the year but each crop did not make intense, precise, and frequent demands on the time of farmers. While subsistence cropping in millet-growing areas does require certain key operations to be performed at certain times, both the length of the seasons and their internal activity structure leave considerable temporal flexibility. This flexibility ceases once major cash crops arrive on the scene, especially onions and peas, but also to some degree sugarcane. The cultivation cycles for the commercial crops crosscut the preexisting calendric cycles which, for most farmers, require room for the basic subsistence crops, and also stretch considerably into the hot season, which was previously a slack period. Furthermore, the vegetable cash crops typically require more intense and carefully timed bursts of activity for weeding, watering, and fertilizer application. Finally, their own cycles of planting and harvesting frequently overlap with each other as well as with those of the main subsistence crops. As a result, especially for those farmers who are self-reliant in terms of family labor, much of the year is a scramble to juggle the cycles of these various crops, and most of them tend to have at least a small amount of their total acreage under some of these cash crops.

As crop seasonalities begin to jostle each other and crowd the time available to many farmers, other periodicities frequently become subordinated to them. Marriage celebrations are frequently timed not solely by reference to auspicious moments, as determined by the Hindu almanac, but must yield to the agricultural schedules of the wealthier families. Pilgrimages once undertaken with great liberality must now be handled more circumspectly, either by going shorter distances, or by staying away fewer days, or by leaving key members of the workforce behind. Major village festivals and rituals seem no longer genuinely to set the pace and structure of the rural calendar, but rather to be islands of cosmological stability amidst an increasingly hurried flow of production-related activities. Even at the everyday level, women frequently find themselves performing important ritual tasks on the run: in the midst of rushing to work on someone's fields, while on the way to get water or firewood, or while tending the family goats or sheep.[7] In short, the traditional interactive rhythm of ritual and ecological periodicities is now increasingly penetrated and framed by the requirements of labor, energy, cash, and demand associated with the commercialization of agriculture. This does not seem to be a temporary shift in the way farmers in Vadi talk about their lives and experience the flow of time, insofar as we can tell by looking at what they say as well as what they do: it looks as if it is not likely to be reversed.

Conclusion

This essay has told a story whose plot has worked at two levels. The first level concerned the evolution of an agronomic discourse in Marathi, in the context of the region. The second level concerned the village of Vadi, and a rather more recent, and detailed, story of technical change in irrigation. It remains now to discuss the general implications of this story, by returning to the main moral issue raised in the introduction to the chapter: how are we to assess the benefits of technological change in such a case?

I suggested that my axiomatic criterion was the *value of reproduction* for any human community. I also suggested that the main requirement for the maintenance of this value was the *reproduction of core values*. By this I meant that our challenge was to establish, in a way that combines our perspectives with the insights of those we study, what core values need to be reproduced for the community itself to be reproduced, not necessarily in an unchanging fashion, but in a way that preserves its distinctive social life.

I believe that there is a set of deep links between agricultural and social life in Vadi, and in communities such as Vadi.[8] These links take many forms, but their critical expression is in a whole variety of what I call *centripetal* social forms. In ritual, in agricultural work, in men's work teams, in women's work teams, in ritualized service-exchange relationships, in relations between rich farmers, between them and poor farmers, and between poorer farmers themselves, there is a rich range of connections, not always determined by ties of caste or kinship, which are

---

7.   The phenomenological situation of poorer rural women is discussed in chapter 4 of this volume.

8.   For a fine exploration of these links, see Schlesinger 1981: 233–74.

enduring, multifunctional, and built on amity. By external criteria, some of these relationships (such as those between landlords and tenants, moneylenders and creditors, richer and poorer farmers) might appear exploitative. But they are crosscut by, and part and parcel of, other modes of interaction to which the language of exploitation would not appear to apply. Together, what these centripetal forms indicate is that the core value of this community is *sociality* itself. That is, though the forms of sociality have changed over time, there is still a widespread sense, instantiated in practice as well as in farmers' talk, that a form of social life built around centripetal pulls is the core value of this community.

It is this core value that is threatened by commercialization, as I have portrayed it in this chapter. At the level of discourse, I have tried to sketch a process that gradually divorces agronomy from agriculture, or, more loosely, divorces agriculture from agrarian relations. More specifically, at the normative heart of the new discourse is a conception of the farmer as a technologically sophisticated, credit-seeking, market-oriented person, whose goals are (in the current commercial sense), to maximize output, profit, and income. Although, particularly in the cultivation of sugarcane, a powerful cooperative movement has emerged in Maharashtra, this does not controvert the general thrust of the new commercializing ideology, which aspires to create a farmer who is free of complex local ties. This is a farmer who responds to *centrifugal* pulls, largely commercial ones, which draw him away from the social demands of village life.

What is true at the macro level of the formation of an agronomic discourse is reflected in a complex way at the level of practice and talk among the farmers of Vadi. As I have suggested in chapter 3 [of this volume], while the small farmers of Vadi are forced to participate in partnership and sharing arrangements if they wish to have any part in the opportunities of commercial agriculture, they do not regard these arrangements as desirable. They aspire to a situation where they might be "big" farmers, who can enter this arena on their own, without recourse to complex sharing arrangements.

It is important here to distinguish cooperation as a *value* from cooperation as a *strategy*. In the traditional set-up, as I have construed it, the prime value of sociality is expressed in a variety of centripetal social forms, many of which involve cooperation. But as the commercialization process of the last century has made its ideological and institutional inroads, the erosion of such centripetal social forms has led to a situation where cooperation has been reduced to a strategy for subsistence.

Particularly for poorer farmers, the aversion to partnership reflects a deep ambivalence about this reduction. They are willing to pursue it, for they see fewer and fewer alternative ways to assure subsistence in the world which they now confront. But they resist it because it is *only* a strategy, furthermore a risky one, and one that does not any more encode or imply broader or deeper social ties. The solution to this ambivalence is, therefore, not simply to create institutions which mediate the conflicts between micromotives and aggregate outcomes (conflicts typified by the prisoner's dilemma). Rather it is to create institutional alternatives to the apparently inexorable march of commercialization. Only such alternatives will restore cooperation as a value, not merely a strategy.

This observation about the reduction of cooperation from a value to a strategy permits me to clarify the relationship between commercialization and individualism in the last century. This relationship has three features: (1) though the relationship between farmers and markets in Western India is far older than the last century, it is now a pervasive factor in more villages and in more transactions in such villages, and it affects more farmers in such villages. There is thus a great increase in the sort of individualism we associate with market-orientation; (2) for some farmers, this has meant the beginnings of a genuinely capitalist orientation to farming, which sees savings, investment, and profit as the goals of agricultural production; (3) for all farmers, rich or poor, social relations in production are increasingly seen as *strategic* interactions with other *individuals* (whether for survival or for profit), rather than as expressions of the values of sociality. This last shift is, in my judgment, the critical differentiating feature of the "individualism" of the last century in rural Western India. Though it is so far visible largely in the domain of production, it will probably soon affect the ethos of consumption as well.

At this point, it may well be asked why the current situation is objectionable. Why can it not be seen as the dawn of a happy world of individualistic, market-oriented, profit-seeking farmers, reorganizing their social lives in keeping with their newfound economic opportunities? There are three answers to this question. The first, which I have already hinted at, is that for many of these farmers, the loss of knowledge (and the associated losses in social ties) that some of these changes bring is a bad risk, since they may well be pushed out of the commercial sphere and pushed back into the subsistence sphere in which such knowledge is not so irrelevant. The second reason is that these changes involve a steady reduction in the relative autonomy of the village as an economic arena, something which on the whole has not been shown to be of either absolute benefit to the nation or to more than a small number of villagers. But the third reason is the most important.

Most small farmers are obsessed with the desire to have a share (even a tiny one) in the market in agricultural commodities not because there is a natural entrepreneurial impulse in everyone, but because *cash* is the key to subsistence to an unprecedented degree in places like Vadi. That is, large-scale transformations in marketing, production, the division of labor, and monetization, have created a situation in which more and more transactions that are critical to subsistence require money. It is this desperate need for money which drives small farmers to push for a tiny piece of the commercial sector in agriculture, even in terribly involuted circumstances. For most of them, such participation in commercial agriculture is not the road to larger capital, growing income, and the status of "big" farmer, but is, rather, the sine qua non of survival in a deeply monetized world.

In this context, there has been a profound transformation of the relationship between risk and sociality in rural life. Where, in the past, partnership arrangements (and sociality in general), of whatever sort, constituted values as well as *hedges against risk*, in the new circumstances of commercialized agriculture, partnerships (and sociality in general) are seen as strategies, as burdens, and indeed as *sources of risk* in agricultural enterprises. Thus, many poorer farmers are in a terrible predicament: they are pressed to participate in a commercial agriculture which pulls them away from a complex web of social ties, yet this pressure generally yields not new wealth but only precarious subsistence in a heavily monetized world. It is this double jeopardy of the centrifugality produced (both ideologically and practically) by the technical needs of commercialization which makes it a dubious proposition, from the point of view of the value of reproduction and the reproduction of values in Vadi.

References

Amin, Shahid. 1982. "Small Peasant Commodity Production and Rural In-debtedness: The Culture of Sugar-cane in Eastern U.P., *c.* 1880–1920." In *Subaltern Studies* I, edited by Ranajit Guha, 39–87. New Delhi: Oxford University Press.

Amruttungal, Ramachandra. 1852. *Jāgtījōt*. Poona: Board of Education.

Appadurai, Arjun. 1981. "Gastro-Politics in Hindu South Asia." *American Ethnologist* 8 (3): 494–511.

———. 1984a. "How Moral is South Asia's Economy?—A review article." *Journal of Asian Studies* 43 (3): 481–97.

———. 1984b. "The Terminology of Measurement in Rural Maharashtra." Manuscript. [A version was published as "Andāj" in *Changing Theory: Concepts from the Global South*, edited by Dilep Menon. London: Routledge India, 2022. A longer version appears as Chapter 1 in this volume.]

———. 1984c. "Wells in Western India: Irrigation and Cooperation in an Agricultural Society." *Expedition* 26 (3): 3–14. [Chapter 3 in this volume.]

———. 1986a. *The Social Life of Things: Commodities in Cultural Perspective.* Cambridge: Cambridge University Press.

———. 1986b. "Is Homo Hierarchicus?" *American Ethnologist* 13 (4): 745-61.

———. 1988. "Putting Hierarchy in Its Place." *Cultural Anthropology* 3 (1): 36–49.

———. 1989a. "Small-Scale Techniques and Large-Scale Objectives." In *Conversations Between Economists and Anthropologists*, edited by Pranab

Bardhan, 250–82. New Delhi: Oxford University Press. [Chapter 2 in this volume.]

———. 1989b. "Transformations in the Culture of Agriculture." In *Contemporary Indian Traditions*, edited by Carla Borden, 173–86. Washington, DC: Smithsonian Institution Press.

———. 1990. "Technology and the Reproduction of Values in Rural Western India." In *Dominating Knowledge: Development, Culture and Resistance*, edited by Frédérique Apffel Marglin and Stephen A. Marglin, 185–216. Oxford: Clarendon Press. [Chapter 5 in this volume.]

———. 1991. "Dietary Improvisation in an Agricultural Economy." In *Diet and Domestic Life in Society*, edited by Anne Sharman, Janet Theophano, Karen Curtis, and Ellen Messer, 207–32. Philadelphia: Temple University Press. [Chapter 4 in this volume.]

Apte, Chintaman Moreshwar. 1890. *Uttama Shētkari*. Akola: Vidharba Press.

Ashok, Rudra, and Pranab Bardhan. 1983. *Agrarian Relations in West Bengal: Results of Two Surveys*. Bombay: Somaiya Publications.

Attwood, Donald W. 1980. *Irrigation and Imperialism: Water Distribution and the Origin of Enclave Capitalism in Rural Western India*. Unpublished ms.

———. 1984. "Capital and the Transformation of Agrarian Class Systems: Sugar Production in India." In *Agrarian Power and Agricultural Productivity in South Asia*, edited by Meghnad Desai, Susanne H. Rudolph, and Ashok Rudra, 20–50. Berkeley: University of California Press.

———. 1992. *Raising Cane: The Political Economy of Sugar in Western India*. Boulder and London: Westview Press.

Balakrishnan, Sai. 2019. *Shareholder Cities: Land Transformations Along Urban Corridors in India*. Philadelphia, PA: University of Pennsylvania Press.

Banaji, Jairus. 1977. "Small Peasantry and Capitalist Domination: Deccan Districts in the Late Nineteenth Century." *Economic and Political Weekly* 12 (33/34): 1375–1404.

Bardhan, Pranab, ed. 1989. *Conversations Between Economists and Anthropologists*. New Delhi: Oxford University Press.

Barth, Fredrik, ed. 1978. *Scale and Social Organization*. Oslo: Universitetsforlaget.

Baudrillard, Jean. 1975. *The Mirror of Production*. Translated by Mark Poster. Candor, NY: Telos Press.

Baviskar, B. S., and Donald Attwood. 1995. *Finding the Middle Path: The Political Economy of Cooperation in Rural India*. Boulder, CO: Westview Press.

Bayliss-Smith, Tim, and Sudhir Wanmali, eds. 1984. *Understanding Green Revolutions: Agrarian Change and Development Planning in South Asia*. Cambridge: Cambridge University Press.

Beteille, André. 1974. *Studies in Agrarian Social Structure*. Oxford: Oxford University Press.

Binswanger, Hans P., and Narpat S. Jodha. 1978. *Manual of Instructions for Economic Investigators in ICRISAT's Village Level Studies*. Hyderabad: ICRISAT.

Bliss, Christopher J., and Nicholas H. Stern. 1982. *Palanpur: The Economy of an Indian Village*. Oxford: Oxford University Press.

Bouglé, Célestin. (1908) 1971. *Essays on the Caste System*. Translated by D. F. Pocock. Cambridge: Cambridge University Press.

Bourdieu, Pierre. 1963. "The Attitude of the Algerian Peasant Toward Time." In *Mediterranean Countrymen: Essays in the Social Anthropology of the Mediterranean*, edited by Julian Alfred Pitt-Rivers, 55–72. Paris: Mouton.

———. 1977. *Outline of a Theory of Practice*. Translated by Richard Nice. Cambridge: Cambridge University Press.

Breman, Jan. 1974. *Patronage and Exploitation: Changing Agrarian Relations in South Gujarat, India*. Berkeley: University of California Press.

Carter, Anthony. 1974. *Elite Politics in Rural India: Political Stratification and Political Alliances in Western Maharashtra*. Cambridge: Cambridge University Press.

Catanach, I. J. 1970. *Rural Credit in Western India, 1875–1930*. Berkeley: University of California Press.

Chambers, Robert. 1983. *Rural Development: Putting the Last First*. London and New York: Longman.

Chambers, Robert, Richard Longhurst, and Arnold Pacey, eds. 1981. *Seasonal Dimensions to Rural Poverty*. London: Frances Pinter.

Charlesworth, Neil. 1985. *Peasants and Imperial Rule: Agriculture and Agrarian Society in the Bombay Presidency, 1850–1933*. Cambridge: Cambridge University Press.

Chaudhari, K. N., and Clive Dewey, eds. 1979. *Economy and Society: Essays in Indian Economic and Social History*. New Delhi: Oxford University Press.

Chayanov, A. V. (1925) 1986. *The Theory of Peasant Economy*. Madison: University of Wisconsin Press.

Cicourel, Aaron V. 1964. *Method and Measurement in Sociology*. New York: Free Press.

———. 1981. "Notes on the Integration of Micro- and Macro-levels of Analysis." In *Advances in Social Theory and Methodology*, edited by Karin Knorr-Cetina and Aaron V. Cicourel, 51–80. Boston and London: Routledge and Kegan Paul.

Collins, Randall. 1981a. "Microtranslation as a Theory-Building Strategy." In *Advances in Social Theory and Methodology*, edited by Karin Knorr-Cetina and Aaron V. Cicourel, 81–108. Boston and London: Routledge and Kegan Paul.

———. 1981b. "On the Microfoundations of Macrosociology." *American Journal of Sociology* 86 (5): 984–1014.

———. 1983. "Micromethods as a Basis for Macrosociology." *Urban Life* 12 (2) (July): 184–202.

Cross, Jamie. 2014. *Dream Zones: Anticipating Capitalism and Development in India*. London: Pluto Press.

Dandekar, V. M. 1981. "On Measurement of Poverty." *Economic and Political Weekly* 16 (July 25): 1241–50.

Das, V., and R. Nicholas. n.d. *Welfare and Well-being in Rural South Asia*. Unpublished paper.

Desai, Meghnad, Susanne Hoeber Rudolph, and Ashok Rudra, eds. 1984. *Agrarian Power and Agricultural Productivity in South Asia*. Berkeley: University of California Press.

Descola, Philippe. 2013. *Beyond Nature and Culture*. Chicago: University of Chicago Press.

Douglas, Mary, ed. 1984. *Food in the Social Order*. New York: Russell Sage Foundation.

Douglas, Mary, and Jonathan Gross. 1981. "Food and Culture: Measuring the Intricacy of Rule Systems." *Social Science Information* 20 (1): 1–35.

Dumont, Louis. 1970. *Homo Hierarchicus: The Caste System and Its Implications*. Chicago: University of Chicago Press.

Durkheim, Émile. 1960. *The Division of Labor in Society*. Translated by George Simpson. Glencoe, IL: Free Press.

Elster, Jon. 1979. *Ulysses and the Sirens: Studies in Rationality and Irrationality*. Cambridge: Cambridge University Press.

Epstein, T. S. 1962. *Economic Development and Social Change in South India*. Manchester: Manchester University Press.

———. 1973. *South India: Yesterday, Today and Tomorrow*. London: Macmillan.

Etienne, Gilbert. 1982. *India's Changing Rural Scene*. New Delhi: Oxford University Press.

Evans-Pritchard, E. E. 1937. *Witchcraft, Oracles and Magic Among the Azande*. Oxford: Oxford University Press.

Farmer, B. H., ed. 1977. *Green Revolution? Technology and Change in New Rice-Growing Areas of Tamil Nadu and Sri Lanka*. London: Macmillan.

Fienberg, S., E. Loftus, and M. Tanur. 1984. "Cognitive Aspects of Health Surveys for Public Information and Policy." Unpublished manuscript.

Foster, George M., Thayer Scudder, Elizabeth Colson, and Robert V. Kemper, eds. 1979. *Long-Term Field Research in Social Anthropology*. New York: Academic Press.

Fukazawa, H. 1983. "Western India." In *The Cambridge Economic History of India, Volume 2, c. 1751–c. 1970*, edited by Dharma Kumar and Meghnad Desai, 177–206. Cambridge: Cambridge University Press.

Geertz, Clifford. 1963. *Agricultural Involution: The Processes of Ecological Change in Indonesia*. Berkeley and Los Angeles: University of California Press.

———. 1973. *The Interpretation of Cultures*. New York: Basic Books.

———. 1975. "Common Sense as a Cultural System." *The Antioch Review* 33 (1): 5–26.

Gibson, Frank K., and Brett W. Hawkins. 1968. "Research Notes: Interviews versus Questionnaires." *American Behavioral Scientist* 12 (1): NS9–NS11.

Giddens, Anthony. 1981. "Agency, Institution and Time-Space Analysis." In *Advances in Social Theory and Methodology*, edited by Karin Knorr-Cetina and Aaron V. Cicourel, 161–74. Boston and London: Routledge and Kegan Paul.

Gough, Kathleen. 1981. *Rural Society in Southeast India*. Cambridge: Cambridge University Press.

Gulati, Leela. 1981. *Profiles in Female Poverty: A Study of Five Poor Working Women in Kerala*. Oxford: Pergamon.

Gupta, Akhil. 1998. *Postcolonial Developments: Agriculture in the Making of Modern India*. Durham, NC: Duke University Press.

Hannerz, Ulf. 1979. "Complex Societies and Anthropology: A Perspective from 1979." *Ethnos* 44 (3/4): 217–41.

Harré, Rom. 1981. "Philosophical Aspects of the Micro-Macro Problem." In *Advances in Social Theory and Methodology*, edited by Karin Knorr-Cetina and Aaron V. Cicourel, 139–60. Boston and London: Routledge and Kegan Paul.

Harriss, Barbara. 1984. *State and Market: State Intervention in Agricultural Exchange in a Dry Region of Tamil Nadu, South India*. New Delhi: Concept Publishing Company.

Harriss, John. 1982. *Capitalism and Peasant Farming: Agrarian Structure and Ideology in Northern Tamil Nadu*. Bombay: Oxford University Press.

———. 1983. "Making Out on Limited Resources: Or What Happened to Semi-feudalism in a Bengal District." In *Papers on the Political Economy of Agriculture in West Bengal*, by John Harriss and Barbara Harriss. Reprint No. 170, School of Development Studies, University of East Anglia. (Reprinted from CRESSIDA Transactions.)

Hill, Polly. 1982. *Dry Grain Farming Families*. Cambridge: Cambridge University Press.

Hirsch, Fred. 1976. *Social Limits to Growth*. Cambridge, MA: Harvard University Press.

Hoy, David, ed. 1986. *Foucault: A Critical Reader*. Oxford: Basil Blackwell.

Hursh-Cesar, Gerald, and Prodipto Roy, eds. 1976. *Third World Surveys: Survey Research in Developing Nations*. Delhi: Macmillan.

Jodha, N. S. 1980. "Intercropping in Traditional Farming Systems." *Journal of Development Studies* 16 (4): 427–42.

———. 1986. "Common Property Resources and Rural Poor in Dry Regions of India." *Economic and Political Weekly* 21 (27) (July 5, 1986): 1169–81.

———. 1989. *Technology Options and Economic Policy for Dryland Agriculture*. New Delhi: Concept Publishing.

Kahneman, Daniel, Paul Slovic, and Amos Tversky, eds. 1982. *Judgment Under Uncertainty: Heuristics and Biases*. Cambridge: Cambridge University Press.

Karve, Irawati K. 1968. *Kinship Organization in India*. Bombay: Asia Publishing House.

Keatinge, Gerald. 1912. *Rural Economy in the Bombay Deccan*. London: Longmans Green.

————. 1921. *Agricultural Progress in Western India*. London: Longmans Green.

Khare, Kasinath Trimbak. 1882. *Hindustānātil Shētkaryānchī Sthithi va Shētkinchi Kāmēn*. Gyanprakash Press.

Khare, R. S. 1976. *The Hindu Hearth and Home*. New Delhi: Vikas.

Knorr-Cetina, Karin. 1981. "The Micro-Sociological Challenge of Macro-Sociology: Towards a Reconstruction of Social Theory and Methodology." In *Advances in Social Theory and Methodology*, edited by Karin Knorr-Cetina and Aaron V. Cicourel, 1–47. Boston and London: Routledge and Kegan Paul.

Knorr-Cetina, Karin, and Aaron V. Cicourel, eds. 1981. *Advances in Social Theory and Methodology*. Boston and London: Routledge and Kegan Paul.

Kumar, Dharma, and Meghnad Desai, eds. 1983. *The Cambridge Economic History of India, Volume 2, c. 1751–c. 1970*. Cambridge: Cambridge University Press.

Kumar, Ravinder. 1968. *Western India in the Nineteenth Century: A Study in the Social History of Maharashtra*. London: Routledge and Kegan Paul.

Leach, Edmund R. 1967. "An Anthropologist's Reflections on a Social Survey." In *Anthropologists in the Field*, edited by D. G. Jogmans and P. C. W. Gutkind, 75–88. New York: Humanities Press.

Leaf, Murray. 1984. *Song of Hope: The Green Revolution in a Punjab Village*. New Brunswick, NJ: Rutgers University Press.

Levien, Michael. 2018. *Dispossession Without Development: Land Grabs in Neoliberal India*. Oxford: Oxford University Press.

Lévi-Strauss, Claude. (1963) 1967. "Introduction: History and Anthropology." In *Structural Anthropology*, 1–28. Translated by Claire Jacobson and Brooke Grundfest Schoep. Garden City, NY: Anchor Books.

Maharashta State. *Season and Crop Report for Maharashtra State for 1975–76*. Department of Agriculture. Maharashtra State: Director, Government Printer and Stationery.

Maine, Henry. 1871. *Village-Communities in the East and West*. London: John Murray,

Mann, Harold H. 1917. *Economic Progress of the Land and Labour in a Deccan Village, No. 1*. London and Bombay: Humphrey Milford, Oxford University Press.

————. 1967. *The Social Framework of Agriculture*. Edited by Daniel Thorner. Bombay: Vora and Co.

Mann, Harold H., and Narayan V. Kanitkar. 1921. *Land and Labour in a Deccan Village, No. 2.* London and Bombay: Humphrey Milford, Oxford University Press.

Marcus, George E., and Dick Cushman. 1982. "Ethnographies as Texts." *Annual Review of Anthropology* 11: 25–69.

Marglin, Frédérique Apffel, and Stephen A. Marglin, eds. 1990. *Dominating Knowledge: Development, Culture, and Resistance.* Oxford: Clarendon Press.

Marriott, McKim, ed. 1955. *Village India: Studies in the Little Community.* Chicago: University of Chicago Press.

———. 1968. "Caste Ranking and Food Transactions: A Matrix Analysis." In *Structure and Change in Indian Society,* edited by Milton Singer and Bernard S. Cohn, 133–71. Chicago: Aldine Publishing.

———. 1976. "Hindu Transactions: Diversity without Dualism." In *Transaction and Meaning: Directions in the Anthropology of Exchange and Symbolic Behavior,* edited by Bruce Kapferer. Philadelphia: Institute for the Study of Human Issues.

Marx, Karl. 1853. "The British Rule In India." *New York Herald Tribune,* June 10, 1853.

Mauss, Marcel. (1925) 1954. *The Gift: Forms and Functions of Exchange in Archaic Societies.* Translated by Ian Cunnison. Glencoe, Illinois: Free Press.

McAlpin, Michelle B. 1983. *Subject to Famine: Food Crises and Economic Change in Western India, 1860–1920.* Princeton, NJ: Princeton University Press.

Mencher, Joan. 1974. "The Caste System Upside Down: Or the Not-So-Mysterious East." *Current Anthropology* 54 (4): 469–93.

———. 1978. *Agriculture and Social Structure in Tamil Nadu: Past Origins, Present Transformations, and Future Prospects.* Durham, NC: Carolina Academic Press.

Merrey, Douglas. 1983. "Watercourse Politics and the Social Organization of Irrigation in a Village in Punjab, Pakistan." Presented on a panel on "Rethinking Agricultural Research for South and Southwest Asia," Annual Meeting of Mid-Atlantic Region of the Association of Asian Studies, October 28–30, 1983, Philadelphia, PA.

Miller, Barbara D. 1981. *The Endangered Sex: Neglect of Female Children in Rural North India.* Ithaca, NY: Cornell University Press.

References

Mitchell, Robert. 1965. "Survey Materials Collected in Developing Countries: Sampling, Measurement and Interviewing Obstacles in Intra- and International Comparisons." *International Social Science Journal* 17: 665–85.

Munro, T. 1806. "Report from the Ceded Districts." Cited in Dumont 1970.

Murtaugh, Michael, and Hugh Gladwin. 1980. "A Hierarchical Decision-Process Model for Forecasting Automobile Type-Choice." *Transportation Research Part A: Policy and Practice* 14 (5/6): 337–48.

Nipunge, H. L., ed. 1981. *Krishival Dāyiri 1981.* Poona: Pusphak Prakashan.

Nisbett, Richard E., and Lee Ross 1980. *Human Inference: Strategies and Shortcomings of Social Judgment.* Englewood Cliffs, NJ: Prentice Hall.

Omvedt, Gail. 1995. *Dalit Visions: The Anti-Caste Movement and the Construction of an Indian Identity.* New Delhi: Orient Longman.

Ortiz, Sutti. 1973. *Uncertainties in Peasant Farming: A Colombian Case.* London: Routledge.

Papanek, Hanna. 1979. "Family Status Production: The 'Work' and 'Non-Work' of Women." *Signs: Journal of Women in Culture and Society* 4 (4): 775–81.

———. 1984. "False Specialization and the Purdah of Scholarship: A Review Article." *Journal of Asian Studies* 44 (1): 127–48.

Perlin, Frank. 1978. "Of White Whale and Countrymen in the Eighteenth Century Maratha Deccan: Extended Class Relations, Rights and the Problem of Rural Autonomy under the Old Regime." *Journal of Peasant Studies* 5 (2): 172–237.

———. 1983. "Proto-Industrialization and Pre-Colonial South Asia." *Past and Present* 98 (1): 30–95.

Rudner, David West. 1994. *Caste and Colonialism in Colonial India: The Nattukottai Chettiars.* Berkeley and Los Angeles: University of California Press.,

Rudra, Ashok. 1984. "Local Power and Farm-level Decision-making." In *Agrarian Power and Agricultural Productivity in South Asia,* edited by Meghnad Desai, Susanne Hober Rudolph and Ashok Rudra, 250–80. Berkeley: University of California Press.

Rudra, Ashok, and Pranab Bardhan. 1983. *Agrarian Relations in West Bengal: Results of Two Surveys.* Bombay: Somaiya.

Quinn, Naomi. 1978. "Do Mfantse Fish-Sellers Estimate Probabilities in Their Heads?" *American Ethnologist* 5 (2): 206–26.

Sahlins, Marshall. 1976. *Culture and Practical Reason*. Chicago: University of Chicago Press.

Saumerez Smith, Richard. 1985. "Rule-by-records and Rule-by-reports: Complementary Aspects of the British Imperial Rule of Law." *Contributions to Indian Sociology*, n.s. 19 (1): 153–76.

Schelling, Thomas C. 1978. *Micromotives and Macrobehavior*. New York: W. W. Norton.

Schlesinger, Lee I. 1981. "Agriculture and Community in Maharashtra, India." In *Research in Economic Anthropology*, Vol. 4, edited by George Dalton, 233–74. Greenwich, CT: JAI Press.

Schuman, Howard, and Stanley Presser. 1981. *Questions and Answers in Attitude Surveys: Experiments on Question Form, Wording and Context*. New York: Academic Press.

Schutz, Alfred. 1970. *Reflections on the Problem of Relevance*. New Haven, CT: Yale University Press.

Sen, Amartya. 1981. *Poverty and Famines: An Essay on Entitlement and Deprivation*. Oxford: Clarendon Press.

Sharma, Ursula. 1980. *Women, Work, and Property in North-West India*. London: Tavistock.

Shrestha, R. 1979. "A Socio-linguistic Appraisal of Survey Questionnaires." In *The Use and Misuse of Social Research in Nepal*, edited by G. Campbell, R. Shrestha, and L. Stone, 71–92. Kathmandu: His Majesty's Government Press.

Slater, Gilbert. 1918. *Some South Indian Villages*. London and New York: Oxford University Press.

Spooner, Brian. 1974. "Irrigation and Society: The Iranian Plateau." In *Irrigation's Impact on Society*, edited by T. E. Downing and McGuire Gibson, 43–57. Anthropological Papers of the University of Arizona, No. 25. Tucson: University of Arizona Press.

Srinivas, M. N. 1959. "The Dominant Caste in Rampura." *American Anthropologist* 61 (1): 1–16.

———. 1976. *The Remembered Village*. Berkeley and Los Angeles: University of California Press.

———. 1979. "Village Studies, Participant Observation and Social Science Research in India." *Economic and Political Weekly* 10 (33, 34 and 35): 1387–94.

Srinivasan, Saradha. 1979. *Mensuration in Ancient India*. Delhi: Ajanta Publications.

Srinivasan, T. K, T. N. Srinivasan, and Pranab K. Bardhan. 1974. *Poverty and Income Distribution in India*. Calcutta: Statistical Publishing House.

Stein, Burton. 1977. "Circulation and the Historical Geography of Tamil Country." *Journal of Asian Studies* 37 (1): 7–26.

Stone, Linda. 1978. "Food Symbolism in Hindu Nepal." *Contributions to Nepalese Studies* 6 (1): 47–65.

Stone, Linda, and G. Campbell. 1984. "The Use and Misuse of Surveys in International Development: An Experiment from Nepal." *Human Organization* 43 (1): 27–37.

Sukhatme, P. V. 1981. "On Measurement of Poverty." *Economic and Political Weekly* 16 (32): 1318–24.

Tambiah, S. J. 1958. "The Structure of Kinship and its Relationship to Land Possession and Residence in Pata Dumbara, Central Ceylon." *Journal of the Royal Anthropological Institute of Great Britain and Ireland* 88 (1): 21–44.

Thompson, E. P. 1967. "Time, Work-Discipline, and Industrial Capitalism." *Past & Present* 38: 56–97.

Zeller, Richard A., and Edward G. Carmines. 1980. *Measurement in the Social Sciences: The Link Between Theory and Data*. New York: Cambridge University Press.

Wallace, Anthony. 1970. *Culture and Personality*, 2nd edition. New York: Random House.

Index

145